CAMBRIDGE NATIONAL

LEVEL 1/2

Information Technologies

Brian Gillinder and Sonia Stuart

DYNAMIC LEARNING

HODDER
EDUCATION
AN HACHETTE UK COMPANY

This resource is endorsed by OCR for use with OCR Level 1/2 Cambridge National Certificate in Information Technologies specification J808. In order to gain OCR endorsement, this resource has undergone an independent quality check. Any references to assessment and/or assessment preparation are the publisher's interpretation of the specification requirements and are not endorsed by OCR. OCR recommends that a range of teaching and learning resources are used in preparing learners for assessment. OCR has not paid for the production of this resource, nor does OCR receive any royalties from its sale. For more information about the endorsement process, please visit the OCR website, www.ocr.org.uk.

Although every effort has been made to ensure that website addresses are correct at time of going to press, Hodder Education cannot be held responsible for the content of any website mentioned in this book. It is sometimes possible to find a relocated web page by typing in the address of the home page for a website in the URL window of your browser.

Hachette UK's policy is to use papers that are natural, renewable and recyclable products and made from wood grown in sustainable forests. The logging and manufacturing processes are expected to conform to the environmental regulations of the country of origin.

Orders: please contact Bookpoint Ltd, 130 Park Drive, Milton Park, Abingdon, Oxon OX14 4SE. Telephone: (44) 01235 827720. Fax: (44) 01235 400401. Email education@bookpoint.co.uk Lines are open from 9 a.m. to 5 p.m., Monday to Saturday, with a 24-hour message answering service. You can also order through our website: www.hoddereducation.co.uk

ISBN: 978 1 5104 2327 5

© Brian Gillinder and Sonia Stuart 2018

First published in 2018 by
Hodder Education,
An Hachette UK Company
Carmelite House
50 Victoria Embankment
London EC4Y 0DZ

www.hoddereducation.co.uk

Impression number 10 9 8 7 6 5 4 3 2

Year   2022 2021 2020 2019 2018

Cover photo © monsitj – stock.adobe.com

Typeset in India

Printed in Dubai

A catalogue record for this title is available from the British Library.

Contents

Learning Outcome 5: To be able to import and manipulate data to develop a solution to meet an identified need

Learning Outcome 6: Understand the different methods of processing data and presenting information

Learning Outcome 7: To be able to select and present information in the development of the solution to meet an identified need

Learning Outcome 8: To be able to iteratively review and evaluate the development of the solution

Answers to the exercises are provided online at www.hoddereducation.co.uk/Product?Product=9781510423275

Acknowledgements

Every effort has been made to trace and acknowledge ownership of copyright. The publishers will be glad to make suitable arrangements with any copyright holders whom it has not been possible to contact. The authors and publishers would like to thank the following for permission to reproduce copyright material.

Page 1 © monsitj/stock.adobe.com; Figure 1.4 © geraldmarella/stock.adobe.com; page 22 © Andrew Stefanovsky/stock.adobe.com; Figures 2.1, 2.2 and 2.3 ProjectLibre; page 37 © Nmedia/stock.adobe.com; Figure 3.1a © Helene Rogers/Art Directors & TRIP/Alamy Stock Photo; Figure 3.1b © Washington Imaging/Alamy Stock Photo; Figure 3.2a © Realimage/Alamy Stock Photo; Figure 3.2b © Carolyn Jenkins/Alamy Stock Photo; Figure 3.5 © phoeilxDE/Shutterstock; page 51 top © Jerome Dancett/Fotolia, second © istockphoto/Oleksiy Mark, third © brentmelissa/istockphoto, bottom © Xuejun li/Fotolia; Figure 3.6 © New photos by Alfonso de Tomas/Alamy Stock Photo; Figure 3.7 © Stephen Frost/Alamy Stock Photo; Figure 3.8 © dclic-photo.fr/stock.adobe.com; Figure 3.9 © Fenton – Fotolia; page 58 © Rawpixel – Fotolia.com; Figure 4.1 © Peter Widmann/Alamy Stock Photo; Figure 4.3 McAfee; Figure 4.12 © B Christopher/Alamy Stock Photo; page 87 © sdecoret/stock.adobe.com; page 119 © pannawat/stock.adobe.com; Figure 6.3 © ZUMA Press Inc/Alamy Stock Photo; Figure 6.4 © TfL, 2017, licensed under the Open Government Licence 3.0; Figure 6.5 © Simon Dack/Alamy Stock Photo; Figure 6.6 © Justin Kase zsixz/Alamy Stock Photo; Figure 6.7 © Michael Ventura/Alamy Stock Photo; Figure 6.8 © Tasha Goddard; Figure 6.9 YouTube and the YouTube Logo are registered trademarks of Google Inc., used with permission; Figure 6.10 © jojje11 – Fotolia; Figure 6.11 © Andrey Popov/stock.adobe.com; page 140 © Rawpixel.com/stock.adobe.com; Figure 7.11 © REDPIXEL/stock.adobe.com; page 157 © Andrew Stefanovskiy/stock.adobe.com.

LO1 Understand the tools and techniques that can be used to initiate and plan solutions

About this chapter

During the life of a project, there are different phases and activities which should be carried out. By completing these activities, the project will have an increased chance of being successful.

A project life cycle should be followed. The life cycle has four phases with each phase having defined tasks to be completed. By following the project life cycle there is less chance of any tasks being missed out, and the deliverable product is more likely to be what the client requires.

One of the activities is to plan the project. Good planning will enable the tasks within the project to be defined, the time required for each task to be calculated and the tasks and the timescale to interlink.

There are many different tools and techniques that can be used during the planning of a project. By knowing about these, you will be able to select and justify the choice of tools and techniques based on the project being planned.

Chapter content

1.1 The phases of the project life cycle and the tasks carried out in each phase
1.2 The interaction and iteration between the phases of the project life cycle
1.3 The inputs and outputs of each phase
1.4 Initial project considerations
1.5 Planning tools and the software types used to develop project plans

1.1 The phases of the project life cycle and the tasks carried out in each phase

The project life cycle

All projects should follow a defined set of phases. By following these phases, it is likely that the final product will be fit for purpose and meet a client's requirements.

There are many different project life cycles. The phases you will learn about in this course are:

- initiation
- planning
- execution
- evaluation.

Figure 1.1 shows how these phases link together.

Figure 1.1 The project life cycle

These are the phases you will need to follow when you are working on your project for R013 Developing technological solutions.

Initiation phase

This is the starting point for a project. It is during this phase that the need for the project is considered.

During this phase, there are some questions which need to be considered and answered. By doing so, it will be possible to see if the project is feasible.

These questions should be considered and answered by people involved in the project. These people should include the client and the **project manager**.

The questions that need to be answered could include:

- What is the end product and who is it for?
- Which people and **resources** will be needed to complete the project?
- What is the timescale for the project and is this realistic?

During this phase, the client will provide a list of requirements or needs that the final product must meet, for example the:

- company logo must be included
- company house style must be used
- age group to be targeted
- format of the output from the final product.

The client may also have constraints or restrictions that should be considered, for example:

- the timescale for the completion of the project
- the budget for the project
- security requirements
- the hardware/software that should be used during the development of the final product
- the hardware/software that the final product should be compatible with.

Key terms

Project manager The person who is in overall charge of the project. They do not carry out any of the development tasks associated with the project but manage the tasks, people and resources needed.

Resources The things needed to complete the project. These may include hardware, software and the different specialist roles such as programmers and testers.

When all the questions have been answered, a feasibility report should be created. The project manager usually creates this. The feasibility report will consider each of the questions and constraints and recommend a way forward. Success criteria and objectives will also be defined within the report. This document will form the basis on which the whole project should be completed.

Any legislative implications will also need to be considered during this phase. For example, if the final product involves storing people's personal details, then the Data Protection Act 1998 will need to be considered. Consideration of the legislative implications during this phase will ensure they are referred to throughout the project life cycle. By doing this, there is a greater probability that the final deliverable product will meet all legislation requirements.

At the end of this phase a review is carried out. This is often called a 'phase review'. This review will make sure that all the questions have been answered and that the client-set constraints are defined. The review will decide if the project is feasible and can move to the next phase. If the decision is that the project is feasible and the review has been fully completed then it is possible to move on to the next phase in the project life cycle.

Planning phase

During this phase, the constraints and requirements included in the feasibility report are used to create detailed project plans. The legislative implications, defined in the initiation phase, will also be considered by the project manager when the project plan is being created.

The designing of the product can be started during this phase. This could include initial designs for a database system, screens for a user interface or initial plans for page plans or web page(s). During this phase, it is also possible that test plans will be created.

The project plan will be used by the project manager to monitor the project's progress.

This is probably the most important phase of the project life cycle. If the plans created by

the project manager during this phase are not detailed enough then the project may not meet the client requirements or the deadline for the project to be completed. It is also possible that the project could go over the budget set by the client. A list of the client-defined constraints is created. This list will be retferred to throughout the project to ensure they are being met.

The project manager will create a project plan using a range of tools and techniques. You will learn about these tools and techniques later in this chapter.

When the project manager is creating the project plan, he or she must define the:

- tasks needed to complete the project
- time needed to complete each task
- **workflow**/linking of tasks
- **contingency** time
- **milestones** and end point
- resources, including specialist staff, needed to complete each task.

Key terms

Workflow What task is dependent on another, what task has to be completed before moving on to the next and which tasks can be completed at the same time as others.
Contingency Time in a project plan that has no tasks assigned. This is used if tasks are not completed on time, to make sure the project still meets the final deadline.
Milestone A given point in time when a task is expected to be started or completed.

When the project plan, test plans, initial designs and the constraints list have been created then a phase review will be carried out. This review will make sure that the project plan is complete and shows that the project can be delivered on time. A decision can be made about carrying on with the project. If the project is feasible in that it can be delivered on time and meet the client requirements and constraints, then the next phase in the project life cycle can begin.

Execution phase

This phase is usually the longest phase in the project life cycle. During this phase, the final product, also known as the deliverable product, is created and tested. The project plan, created in the planning phase, is used by the project manager and team to identify the tasks that need to be carried out.

The project manager will use the project plan to monitor the project and to identify any possible issues relating to time, budget and specialist staff. The project manager will also monitor the quality of the tasks being carried out. It is easier to correct any issues during this phase than it is when the final product has been completed.

The plan will be used to monitor and mitigate other risks associated with the project. These risks can include security, ethical, moral and regulations/legislation.

During the life of a project it is possible that regulations and legislation may change or be amended. By considering these throughout the life cycle, the risk of the deliverable product not meeting current regulations and legislation will be reduced.

During the final part of this phase, the deliverable product should be tested. The product should be tested using the test plans created during the planning phase and against the client's requirements and constraints. In some projects, testing may have been carried out during the creation of the product.

During this phase, most of the planned tasks will be completed. The output from this phase is the final or deliverable product being ready for the final review. If the planning has been detailed enough then the product will be completed on time, within the agreed budget and will meet all the client requirements.

When the deliverable product has been completed and tested, then a phase review will be carried out. This review will confirm that the project is complete and all the tasks have been successfully completed. The project can then move on to the final phase in the project life cycle – the evaluation phase.

Evaluation phase

This is the final phase in the project life cycle. It is during this phase that the deliverable product is released to the client and user documentation created. The user documentation will include installation and user guides.

These will be used by the client to ensure the deliverable product can be successfully used and that if any problems occur, they can be rectified. The installation guide will be used to ensure that the deliverable product can be reinstalled in case of any hardware upgrades.

The review during this phase focuses on the overall project including the deliverable product and will cover:

- the success of the project measured against success criteria and user requirements which were created in the initiation phase
- any deviations from original plans
- the effect of processes and resources on creating the deliverable product, for example software selected, tools and techniques used, compatibility between software and systems
- maintainability, which includes any future development of the product in terms of the use of emerging technologies or adapting to any changes in the client's business or organisation.

When this review has been completed, the deliverable product and user documentation are passed to the client.

 Activity

One project that didn't meet the defined requirements was the software update to the Nest Smart thermostat in January 2016. Investigate other projects that went wrong after they had been installed or failed to meet the defined constraints of time or budget.

The advantages of following a project life cycle

There are many advantages of following a project life cycle.

- The project life cycle provides a structured approach for the project. This allows everyone working on the project to see how the project is progressing. There are clearly defined tasks which must be completed within each phase.
- There are defined inputs and outputs for each phase. These form part of the interaction between each phase. You will learn about the interaction between the phases later in this chapter.
- The roles and responsibilities of each member of the project team are clearly defined so each person knows the task they are working on.
- Resources can be allocated in advance so that any issues can be dealt with at the start of the project rather than during a task. The resources include people, hardware and software.
- The project manager can monitor the progress of the project. They will know when each task and phase has been completed. This allows the project manager to make sure the project is on time and that the final deliverable product will be delivered on time to the client.
- The end-of-phase reviews can be carried out to make sure that the project is meeting the success criteria, objectives and client-defined constraints. The end-of-phase reviews will increase the client's confidence that the final deliverable product will meet their needs.

Practice questions

1 Identify **two** tasks that are carried out during the planning phase. [2 marks]
2 Identify the phase of the project life cycle in which user documentation is created. [1 mark]
3 Describe **two** advantages of following a project life cycle. [4 marks]
4 Discuss the implications to a project if the project life cycle is not followed. [10 marks]

1.2 The interaction and iteration between the phases of the project life cycle

Each phase of the project life cycle interacts with the phases before and after it. Figure 1.2 shows the **interaction** between the phases. You can see that there is no interaction between the evaluation and initiation phases. This is because the evaluation phase is the final phase of the project life cycle. When this phase has been finished then the project has been completed.

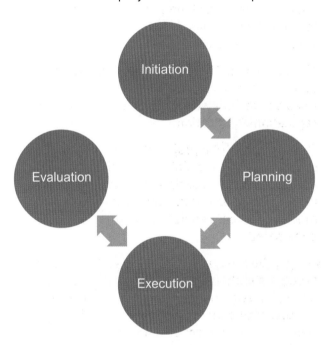

Figure 1.2 The interaction between the phases of the project life cycle

Each phase has defined outputs. These outputs are the inputs for the next phase of the project life cycle. You will learn about the inputs and outputs of each phase later in this chapter.

If any of the tasks within a phase have not been successfully completed then it is not possible to move on to the next phase. The project might have to return to the previous phase if any information is missing.

For example, if during the planning phase it is found that not all of the client's requirements have been defined, then the planning phase must stop and the project must return to the initiation phase. This is an example of **iteration** between the initiation and planning phases.

The main points about iteration and interaction between the phases of the project life cycle are that they can:

- occur between all the phases of the project life cycle, except between the evaluation and initiation phases, because when a project has reached and finished the evaluation phase, then the project has finished.
- only occur between any given phase and the phase before or after, except the evaluation phase, as there is no phase after it.

Key terms

Interaction How the phases link together.

Iteration The repeating of a phase. Each repetition of a phase, when amendments will be made, is called an iteration. The results of an iteration are used as the starting point of the next.

Table 1.1 The interaction and iteration between the phases

Phase	Interaction with	Iteration with
Initiation	Planning	
Planning	Initiation Execution	Initiation
Execution	Planning Evaluation	Planning
Evaluation	Execution	Execution

Practice questions

1. Which phases interact with the planning phase? [2 marks]
2. Explain why there is no interaction between the evaluation and initiation phases. [3 marks]
3. Explain what would happen if any of the tasks in a phase were not completed. [3 marks]

1.3 The inputs and outputs of each phase

One of the advantages of following a project life cycle is that each phase has clearly defined inputs and outputs. These inputs and outputs form some of the interactions between the phases.

Table 1.2 The inputs and outputs for each phase of the project life cycle

	Inputs	Outputs
Initiation	User requirements User constraints	Feasibility report Legislation implications Phase review
Planning	Feasibility report Legislation implications	Project plan Test plan Constraints list Phase review
Execution	Project plan Test plan Constraints list	Deliverable product Test results Phase review
Evaluation	Deliverable product Test results	Release of deliverable product User documentation Final evaluation report

Top tip

You will need to select and use the appropriate inputs and outputs for each phase of your project for R013.

User requirements

The user requirements form part of the input to the initiation phase. The user requirements define what the client wants the product to achieve.

The requirements may be generic, for example:

- keeping records about suppliers
- producing reports about the most popular products
- the website must have ten linked web pages.

When the product is being created during the execution phase, these generic requirements will be used by the development team, who will use their skills to create a product that meets the requirements.

Some requirements may be specific, for example:

- the reports that are generated by the product must fit onto the company headed paper
- the length of the video to be embedded in the product must be three minutes and it must include the company contact details at the end
- all queries in the product must require user input
- the company logo must appear on every screen/slide/web page/report etc.

It is important to remember that a client may not have the specialist skills needed to clearly define the requirements for a product and that they are not really bothered how the requirement is met as long as it is. The client will liaise with the project manager to discuss the user requirements of the product.

The user requirements form part of the input to the initiation phase.

User constraints

These are given to the project manager by the client and form part of the input to the initiation phase. The constraints are restrictions which the project manager must stick to during the project life cycle. There are four constraints.

- Timescale: The start and end dates for the project. The end date is when the deliverable product is released to the client.
- Budget: The amount of money that can be spent during the project. If the project is planned in enough detail then the budget should not be exceeded. There are, however, always exceptions to this.
- Hardware: The hardware that the client wants the deliverable product to be installed or run on. The hardware to be used during the creation of the product may also be defined by the client.
- Software: The software that the client wants the deliverable product to run on. The software to be used during the creation of the product may also be defined by the client.

The user constraints form part of the input to the initiation phase.

Feasibility report

The feasibility report includes the answers to all the questions that are asked during the initiation phase. The report can also include different solutions for the client. The client can then select the solution they would like to be created.

The feasibility study will also consider the constraints and requirements which have been provided by the client. These need to be realistic if the project is to go ahead. If any of the requirements or constraints are not realistic, then the project manager can liaise with the client to create new requirements and constraints.

The final part of the feasibility study is the answer to the question 'Should the project go ahead?'

The feasibility report forms part of the input for the planning phase.

Group discussion

In a small group, each person should identify two questions that could be answered in the feasibility report that will be created for a spreadsheet recording the results of a football tournament. In your group, discuss each question and its usefulness for a feasibility report.

Legislation implications

Legislation implications need to be considered at the start of the project. Which Acts, legislation and regulations need to be considered will depend on the type of product that is to be created, for example:

- If a website is to be created, then the project manager may need to consider the Copyright, Designs and Patents Act 1988, if any images or photographs created by other people are to be used.
- If a database is to be created which holds people's personal contact details, then the Data Protection Act 1998 (DPA) will need to be considered by the project manager.

The legislation implications form part of the input for the planning phase.

Phase review

The phase review for the initiation phase will consider the feasibility report. A decision will be taken by the project manager and the client about whether the project is to carry on. The phase review for the initiation phase may find some omissions in the information collected and so the initiation phase will be repeated.

The phase review forms part of the input for the planning phase.

Project plan

The project plan, as has already been covered in this chapter, is created by the project manager. The plan forms the basis on which the project will be completed. The plan will include:

- a breakdown of the tasks, and the time and resources allocated to each one
- how the tasks link – it may be possible to complete some tasks at the same time while others will need to be completed one after another
- milestones and end date of the project.

The project plan forms one of the outputs from the planning phase and one of the inputs for the execution phase.

Test plan

Test plans may be created during the planning phase. The test plans, at this phase, will be mainly concerned with the testing of the user requirements to ensure all requirements have been met. It may also be possible, depending on the product to be created, to produce a test plan to be used during the creation of the product.

For example, if a database is to be created, then the test plan could cover the names of the tables and fields which are to be used.

The test plans form one of the outputs from the planning phase and one of the inputs for the execution phase.

Constraints list

The constraints list is created from the user constraints provided by the client in the initiation phase. The list provides detailed information about each of the constraints. This is usually a document which is constantly referred to during the project life cycle. It is referred to during the phase reviews to make sure that all the constraints are met.

It is important to keep referring to these. If any of the constraints cannot be met, it is better that this is found out at the start of the project, when a solution can be found, rather than when the product has been created.

The constraints list forms one of the outputs from the planning phase and one of the inputs for the execution phase.

Phase review

The phase review for the planning phase will consider the completed plan, test plans and the constraints list. It is important that all these documents are detailed, containing as much information as possible.

Each of these documents will be considered by the project manager to check there are no omissions. If any omissions are found then the planning phase may have to be redone. Any issues that are identified during the phase review will need to be resolved, with a plan for resolving these issues put into place.

If serious omissions are found, the project may need to return to the initiation phase. This would be an example of iteration between the initiation and planning phases.

The plan should include all the tasks and resources required to complete the project as well as the milestones, including the end date which should be defined and agreed with the client.

When the plan, test plans and constraints list have been checked and agreed by the client, it will be possible to move to the execution phase of the project life cycle.

The phase review forms the final part of the output from the planning phase and one of the inputs to the execution phase.

Deliverable product

During the execution phase, the product is created. By the end of the execution phase, the product should have been created and tested. If any bugs or errors are found with the product during testing then it is during this phase that these are corrected. Retests will be carried out to ensure the product works as intended and meets the defined client or user requirements.

The deliverable product forms one of the outputs from the execution phase and one of the inputs for the evaluation phase.

Test results

The product will be tested during the execution phase. These tests will be carried out both during creation and when it has been completed. The results of the testing will be recorded and checked to make sure that every part of the product has been tested. The test plans used will be those created during the planning phase and those created during the execution phase. The results of any retests will also be recorded.

The test results form one of the outputs from the execution phase and one of the inputs for the evaluation phase.

Links to other sections

You will learn more about the structure of a test plan in Chapter 2.

Phase review

The phase review for the execution phase will consider the completed deliverable product, the constraints list and the results of the testing. The plan will have been monitored throughout the execution phase by the project manager to ensure that the project is on track and on time. It may be that the built-in contingency time has had to be used to ensure that the project will be completed by the final deadline. As with the phase review in the planning phase, any issues that are identified during the phase review will need to be resolved, with a plan for resolving these issues put into place.

The deliverable product will be reviewed against the test results, the user requirements and the constraints list. If the product meets all of these then it is signed off as being fit for release to the client. If the product does not meet all of these then the execution phase may need to be redone. If the project manager has been closely monitoring the project during the execution phase then it is likely that the deliverable product will be fit for purpose and ready to release to the client.

The phase review is the final output from the execution phase and one of the inputs for the evaluation phase.

Release of deliverable product

When the created product has been completed during the execution phase, it has to be fully checked before it is delivered to the client. The product will be checked against the constraints list and the defined requirements. User documentation will be created while someone actually uses the product. The product will also be installed onto the client's computer system where it will be checked again to make sure it is fully working as intended.

When the project team is happy with the deliverable product, it is released to the client. Releasing the deliverable product to the client is part of the output from the evaluation phase.

User documentation

When the product has been completed, user documentation needs to be created and passed to the client. The user documentation may take the form of:

- a user guide showing how to use the product
- an installation guide, which could be used in the future if the product needs to be reinstalled
- test plans showing the results of tests carried out both during creation and after the product had been completed
- security details which will show the built-in security and how to set up, for example, new users with access details.

There are many different types of user documentation. Which type is passed to the client will depend on the product being created. The user documentation is part of the output from the evaluation phase.

Activity

Using the table below, fill in the type of user documentation that might be passed to the client for the defined products.

You may need to add more rows to the table.

Database	Multi-media Product	Website	Spreadsheet

Final evaluation report

The final evaluation considers all aspects of the project throughout all the phases of the project life cycle. The final review will need to:

- measure success against criteria/objectives
- review deviations from original plans including whether the project has delivered the final product to the client on schedule
- evaluate the effect of processes and resources on delivering solutions, e.g. software selected, tools and techniques used, compatibility between software and systems
- assess the maintainability, e.g. further development of the system, adoption of emerging technologies, adapting to a changed environment.

Practice questions

1 Identify and describe **two** user constraints.
   [4 marks]

2 Identify **one** input into the evaluation phase. [1 mark]

3 A user guide is one type of user documentation which may be created during the evaluation phase. Identify and describe **two** other types of user documentation. [6 marks]

1.4 Initial project considerations

One of the tasks which will be carried out during the initiation phase is to set the objectives for the project.

It is important that these objectives are clearly defined because clear and achievable objectives will help during the project. Clearly defined objectives will also help to ensure that the final product meets the needs of the client and ensure that the project is successful.

There are many different types of considerations which need to be thought about during the initiation phase. Which types of objective are used and developed will depend on the type of product to be created.

The main types of objective are:

- SMART goals
- user requirements
- success criteria
- constraints/limitations, i.e. time, resources, regulations, security/risk management, mitigation of risks.

SMART goals

SMART stands for:

Specific **M**easurable **A**chievable **R**ealistic **T**ime

- **S**pecific: At the start of a project, the client will usually only have a general idea of the type of product they need creating. During the initiation phase, the project manager and client will discuss the general idea to get more details.

  By gaining more detail about the product, there is a greater chance of the final product meeting the needs of the client.

  The clearer the specific goals are, the easier it will be to monitor the project through the life cycle and measure the success or failure during the phase reviews.

- **M**easurable: Each goal set must be measurable. This will allow the project manager to look at the project during each phase review to make sure that the measurable goals are being achieved.

- **A**chievable: The goals set must be achievable. This means that it is possible to create the product that the client requires in the time scale. If goals are set which are not achievable, then this may cause the project to fail, with the deliverable product not meeting the client requirements.

- **R**ealistic: The goals set must be realistic. This means that the project manager and the project team believe that the goals set can be achieved. A realistic goal is one which the project manager and team are able to work towards and achieve.

- **T**ime: Setting a time scale is essential. Without a clear and defined time scale then the project could just keep going and maybe not achieve what the client wants.

The time scale set in the initiation phase will form the basis for the project manager to create the project plan. The time scale can be taken from the client's defined end date, that is, when the product needs to be delivered by.

By setting this date, the project manager will know how long the project is to last. This will help when allocating the time for each task in the project plan.

SMART goals overlap and interlink. Figure 1.3 shows how each goal overlaps with others.

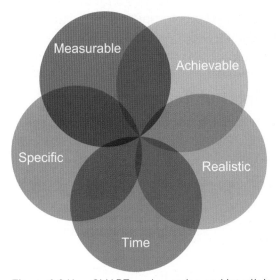

Figure 1.3 How SMART goals overlap and interlink

 Activity

Create SMART goals for a piece of coursework you have to complete.

Join with another person or group and evaluate each other's SMART goals.

User requirements

Links to other sections

You have already learned about user requirements earlier in this chapter, in Section 1.1.

The user requirements need to be defined and used during the initiation phase. It is important that during each phase review, the requirements are referred to as part of the monitoring of the project by the project manager. If it is found that the user requirements are not being met, then changes to the product must be made to ensure that all user requirements *are* met.

Success criteria

The project needs to be measured against a list of criteria to see if it has been successful. The starting point for creating success criteria should be taken from the client requirements about what the final product needs to do or include, or what the inputs and outputs are.

If success criteria are not clearly defined then how can the project be measured for being successful?

Success criteria should be measurable. This will allow them to be part of the phase reviews and help to check that the project, and product, will meet the requirements. The success criteria should also be realistic and relevant.

The success criteria should be realistic because if they are not, the project will probably fail when measured against the success criteria. The success criteria should be relevant, because if they have no relevance to the product being created, then the project will not meet those criteria.

Without success criteria which are relevant and/or realistic, the project is being set up to fail!

One success criterion which must always be created relates to the time for the project to be completed within. This is important because if the project is not completed within the time constraint, usually defined by the client, then the project could be considered to be a failure.

Using time as a success criterion will allow the project manager to create a realistic project plan which will then be monitored throughout the project and during the phase reviews.

Success criteria could include generic criteria such as:

Original images should be used.

While this is a valid generic success criterion, it should be more specific: related to the product being created. This generic criterion can be made more specific by, for example, changing it to:

Include two original images of sailing boats on Lake Windermere.

This criterion is specific and can be measured during the project.

For example, if the product is to advertise sailing on Lake Windermere then the generic criterion could be met with an image of a dog in a field, while the specific criterion would ensure an image which is relevant to the product being created.

Figure 1.4 Does the image meet the success criteria?

Other success criteria, depending on the product to be created, could include:

- target audience
- colours/font to be used
- hardware platform the product is to be installed on
- the software that is to be used during creation for the product and/or the user documentation
- how the product is to be accessed, for example, through a network or via the cloud
- components to be used
- input and output format and contents.

Activity

You have been asked to create a presentation for the maths department to be shown at a GCSE open evening. The presentation will run automatically and when it has finished will loop back to the beginning. The presentation should last between 3.5 and 4 minutes.

The maths department has asked that images of each teacher and classroom are included. Information about GCSE Maths and some example maths questions, with answers, should be shown in the last part of the presentation.

The presentation should use the school colours, use the same font throughout and be based on at least one template.

Develop the success criteria for this presentation.

Constraints/limitations

Some of the constraints will have been provided by the client. You have already learned about user constraints earlier in this chapter, in Section 1.1.

The user constraints usually cover:

- time
- resources such as budget, hardware and software.

There are other constraints which should be considered during the initiation and planning phases of the project life cycle. These include:

- regulations
- security/risk management
- mitigation of risks.

Regulations include current legislation such as the Data Protection Act 1998 and the Copyright, Designs and Patents Act 1988, as well as health and safety legislation. The legislation and regulations that will have to be considered when initiating and planning a project will depend on the product being created.

For example, if a website is to be created, then the Copyright, Designs and Patents Act 1988 will need to be considered. This is because images may be taken from third-party sources. If this happens then the images may be copyrighted. This means that permission to use the image needs to be sought from the creator of the image. If the images are used without this permission being given, then the Copyright, Designs and Patents Act 1988 has been broken.

Links to other sections

You will learn more about the relevant legislation in Chapter 4, Section 4.5.

Security management includes logical and physical protection.

Logical protection methods are methods which are computer-based that can be put in place by the development team or the network/system administrator. During the initiation and planning phases, the client and project manager will discuss what data is to be stored. If data needs to be secured by logical protection methods, then the design of these methods will become a task in the project plan.

Logical protection methods are put in place to reduce or mitigate the risks to the data being stored, for example, preventing the stored data from being accessed, edited or deleted.

Logical protection methods can include:

- firewalls
- encryption
- access rights
- user names and passwords.

Logical protection methods can also be used to conform to regulations and legislation. For example, if people's personal data is being stored, the protection methods used should conform to the Data Protection Act 1998. One of the principles of the DPA is to keep data secure. The use of logical protection methods to access data can increase the security of the data.

Physical protection methods are put in place to stop unauthorised people physically getting to the computer system.

Physical protection methods can include:

- locking rooms that the computer equipment is located in
- bolting computers to desks
- device locks
- using and closing blinds at windows.

Physical protection methods are usually recommended by the project team but are implemented by the client when the deliverable product has been released.

Links to other sections

You will learn more about physical and logical protection methods in Chapter 4, Section 4.4.

Mitigation of risks

During the life of any project, setbacks or problems can occur. Risk mitigation refers to the steps that can be taken to reduce the impact of these setbacks or problems. If these are not reduced then the impact could result in a delay in delivering the final product to the client.

One of the most common types of risk that can occur is technical risk. This type of risk is related to the equipment, hardware and software that are being used during the project. A technical risk can also apply to the people who are involved in the project.

One way of reducing technical risk is to create procedures that must be followed. These could include:

- file and folder naming conventions
- version control of the files and folders that are created and used
- the processes for creating and storing back-ups of files and folders.

Regular meetings with the project team can also help to mitigate risk, as potential problems can be discussed, with plans being put into place before the problem happens.

Complex tasks could be divided between team members. This could mean that if a technological problem arose then only a small part of the project would be affected.

Careful scheduling of tasks using planing tools can also mitigate risk.

Links to other sections

You will learn about how Gantt and PERT charts can be used when planning a project in Section 1.5 of this chapter.

One of the features of these planning tools is contingency time. With contingency time built into a project, if a problem occurs this time can be used for solving the problem. Building this time into the project plan means that the final product will be delivered to the client on the agreed date.

The purpose and importance of setting objectives

It is very important that the project manager and client set objectives. These objectives will form the basis for the project and the final deliverable product will be measured against them.

The objectives will be examined during the phase reviews. If during a phase review it is found that the objectives are not being met, then the project must be stopped. The project may return to the previous phase, an iteration, to solve the problem. Once the problem has been solved then the project can start again.

If correct objectives are set then:

- the product will fully meet the defined client requirements
- nothing will be left out so the product can be used as soon as it is ready
- the product will be delivered within the agreed timescale.

Activity

In pairs, think about what could happen if incorrect objectives are set for a project.

Create a document and present your findings to the rest of the class.

Practice questions

1 Explain why success criteria should be measurable. [3 marks]
2 Give **two** reasons why it is important to set objectives. [6 marks]

1.5 Planning tools and the software types used to develop project plans

Planning tools

During the planning phase, the project manager will use planning tools to create documentation to help during the creation of the product. Some types of plans can be used during the project to monitor the project.

Some types of plans can also be used during the phase reviews to make sure the project is running as it was planned. These project plans will show the tasks, the time allocated to each task, the task dependencies, and milestones.

Other types of planning tools can be created to show the tasks, or processes, which may have to be completed during the creation of the product. And some can help to create initial designs for the final product.

There are many types of planning tools. Which type of tool or tools will be used during the planning phase will depend on the type of product that is to be created. It may be better to create some plans by hand. This means that the plans can be changed easily while they are being created and it is sometimes better to put down initial planning ideas on paper.

Planning tools include:

- Gantt charts
- PERT (Project Evaluation and Review Technique)
- critical path
- visualisation diagram
- flow charts
- mind map
- task list.

Table 1.3 Tools can be divided into formal and informal planning tools

Formal	Informal
Gantt chart	Flow chart
PERT chart	Mind map
Critical path	Task list
Visualisation diagram	

Top tip

You will need to be able to select and use planning tools to create a plan for your project for R013. In preparation for your exam you will need to know the different components of each planning tool and how they can be used to create plans.

Gantt charts

A **Gantt** chart shows each task as a block of time and indicates:

- how long each task should take
- the order in which the tasks should be completed
- **dependencies** between tasks
- milestones
- contingency time.

You can see in Table 1.4 the start of planning for a project. In this example, the initiation

and planning phases have been broken down into tasks. The proposed start and end dates have been defined, as has the duration of each task.

You can see that the tasks of constructing the test plans and the constraints list will be happening at the same time as the task of planning. This is an example of **concurrent** tasks.

Key terms

Gantt chart A visual method of showing the proposed timing of each task needed to complete a project.
Dependency A dependent task is one that cannot be started until a previous, specified task has been completed.
Concurrent Tasks which can be completed at the same time.

Table 1.4 The task list

Task	Start Date	End Date	Duration
Gather requirements	01-Mar	04-Mar	3
Legislation implications	06-Mar	10-Mar	4
Feasibility report	12-Mar	20-Mar	8
Phase review	21-Mar	22-Mar	1
Planning	24-Mar	12-Apr	19
Create constraints list	03-Apr	12-Apr	9
Create test plans	09-Apr	12-Apr	3
Phase review	14-Apr	15-Apr	1

You can also see some contingency time that has been proposed. One of these is where the end date of the initiation phase review is day 21, but the planning does not start until day 24. This allows two days' contingency time between the end of the initiation phase and the start of the planning phase.

This table can now be created as a Gantt chart. This is shown in Figure 1.5. The triangles show the milestones. You will see one at the end of each phase review.

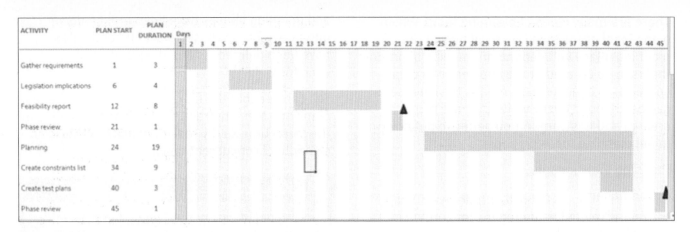

Figure 1.5 The Gantt chart

Activity

Identify the contingency times that have been built in to the project plan.

Think about why this contingency time has been built in. Think about the possible implications to the project if there was no contingency time.

PERT

PERT stands for **P**roject **E**valuation and **R**eview **T**echnique. A PERT chart looks a bit like the visualisation of a railway map.

The PERT chart uses circles, or rectangles, to represent tasks or milestones. The circles or rectangles are sometimes called nodes.

Lines are drawn between these circles to represent dependent tasks and the time allocated to them. Two lines can come out of any event to represent tasks that can be done concurrently.

The PERT chart in Figure 1.6 represents the task plan in Table 1.4

Key term

PERT Program Evaluation Review Technique.

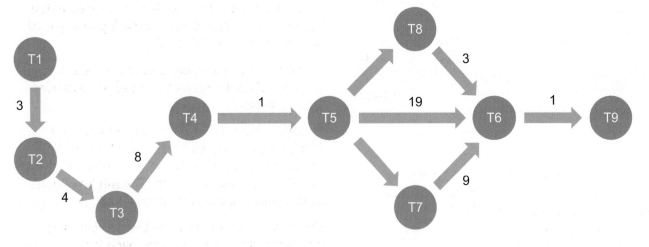

Figure 1.6 The PERT chart

The PERT chart can be used by the project manager to show the critical path.

Critical path

The **critical path** is the longest path that the project should take to be completed. The critical path analyses the tasks that are dependent and works out the time taken to complete all of these.

This path shows the shortest time that a project can be completed in, if all goes to plan.

If we look back at the task list in Table 1.4, we can see that the critical path for the initiation and planning phases will be 45 days.

This is taken from adding up the allocated time for all the dependent, not concurrent, tasks, including contingency time.

The critical path can be used by the project manager to monitor the project to make sure every task is running to schedule.

Key term

Critical Path The sequence of tasks that shows the shortest time taken for completion of a project

Practice questions

1 Explain what is meant by a dependent task.
[3 marks]
2 Explain why contingency time should be built into a project plan. [3 marks]
3 Identify two components of a PERT chart.
[2 marks]

Visualisation diagrams

A visualisation diagram is a rough drawing or sketch of what the final product will look like. The diagram can be used to visually plan the layout of an image. This diagram is usually used when a static product is being created.

A static product is one that doesn't move and examples include:

- a CD/DVD/Blu-ray™ cover
- a poster for a film or advert
- a web page/multimedia page layout
- a magazine front cover or an inside advert.

A visualisation diagram cannot be used for anything that has a timeline, such as a video.

These diagrams can also be used to show the format and layout of any outputs, for example a report.

A visualisation diagram can also be created to help people, usually the client, to understand numerical data. The most common type of visualisation diagram for numerical data is a graph or chart.

There are many benefits of using a visualisation diagram to show data. The most common ones are that:

- information and data can be understood quickly
- emerging trends and patterns can be spotted quickly
- non-specialists can understand the data/numbers being shown.

Flow chart

A flow chart can be used to show the steps, decisions and outputs in a process, for example, how the discount on an order can be calculated. You will have learned about creating this type of flow chart in your KS3 study.

A flow chart can also be used to create a simple diagram of all the steps that need to be carried out in a project.

When planning a project, or part of a project, using a flow chart, each task is set out in the proposed sequence – the order in which the tasks have to be completed. Each task will lead to the next, displaying the sequence of tasks.

Unlike some other planning tools, there is no indication of the timescale for each task.

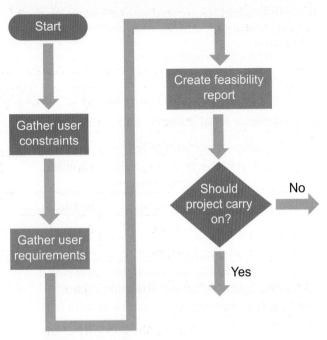

Figure 1.7 A flow chart

The flow chart in Figure 1.7 shows some of the tasks which are carried out during the initiation phase. The diamond shape shows the 'Go, No Go' decision that is made at the end of the phase to see whether the project can move to the next phase.

Some flow chart rules
- The flow chart must begin with 'Start' and end with 'Finish'.
- Each task should be listed in a rectangular box.
- The diamond shape is used for decisions and should have two outputs:
  - Yes: Continue to next phase/task
  - No: Return to previous phase (iteration).

Activity

Using the task list in Table 1.4, create a flow chart to show the sequence of tasks and decisions taken.

Mind map

A mind map could also be called a spider diagram.

Mind maps start with a target or goal. This is sometimes known as a central idea or node.

To achieve the target, lots of other tasks and activities need to be completed. Even the biggest and most complicated project is made up of lots of little tasks.

The tasks are linked to the target by lines or arrows. These can also be known as branches. Each branch could have a word on it. It is also possible to use an image or drawing. Each branch may have other smaller tasks coming off it.

If you look at part of a mind map, Figure 1.8, you will see that the target is to redecorate a bedroom. The main branches coming off that show the main tasks to be completed. For example, remove the old wallpaper. You can then see that a sub-task of this is to hire a wallpaper stripper machine.

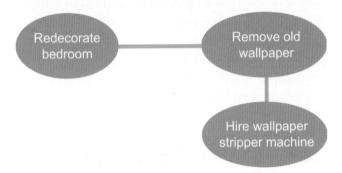

Figure 1.8 A mind map

Mind map software may be available in your centre.

Activity

Complete the mind map shown in Figure 1.8 to show all the tasks related to the target of redecorating a bedroom.

Task list

Task lists show which tasks have to be completed, the start and end dates and the duration, i.e. how long each task should take. A task list is shown in Table 1.4.

A task list should include all the tasks that must be completed during a project. Some of the tasks will be large tasks which will need breaking down into sub-tasks. For example, if you look at the task list in Table 1.4 you will see that one of the tasks to be completed is to gather requirements.

This task could be broken down into sub-tasks. These sub-tasks might include 'gather user requirements and user constraints'.

A task list should be in a logical order so the tasks flow from the initiation phase to the end of the evaluation phase. This is a little bit like the process for developing a Gantt chart. Every task must be defined in order of when it has to be completed.

Some task lists, like the example in Table 1.4, may have start dates and include how much time should be taken to complete the task. By listing these, monitoring of the project can take place because the project manager will be able to see what tasks should have been completed by when and thus if the project is falling behind schedule.

It is also possible to define the resources that will be needed for each task or sub-task.

Activity

Produce a task list for organising a class trip to The Victoria and Albert Museum in London.

Components of planning tools

Each planning tool has different components. These components can be linked to create a project plan.

Table 1.5 The components for Gantt charts, PERT charts and visualisation diagrams

Gantt chart	PERT chart	Visualisation diagrams
Date/days along the top	Nodes/sub-nodes	Multiple images/ graphics
Tasks down the left side	Time/duration lines	Size and position of images/graphics
Blocks to represent the time each task is allocated	Task sequences	Position and style of text
Milestones as diamonds/triangles	Dependent tasks	Fonts
Dependent tasks	Concurrent tasks	Annotations
Concurrent tasks	Can show critical path	Colours/themes

Flow charts, mind maps and task lists have fewer components. These are sometimes viewed as informal planning tools but are just as important as Gantt or PERT charts and visualisation diagrams.

Table 1.6 Components in flow charts, mind maps and task lists

Flow chart	Mind map	Task list
Start point	Nodes	Tasks
End point	Sub-nodes	Sub-tasks
Decisions	Branches/ connecting lines	Start date
Processes	Key words	End date
Connecting lines	Colours	Duration
Direction arrows	Images	Resources

Advantages and disadvantages of planning tools

Table 1.7 on the next page shows some of the strengths and weaknesses of each planning tool. The choice of project planning tools will depend on the project being completed. If a planning tool is used that is not appropriate or useful then, in some cases, this is worse than having no plan at all.

Types of software used

During the creation of the project plan, the project manager will use software. Different types of software can be used. The type of software chosen will depend on the type of planning that is being created. The types of software that could be used include:

- project management software
- spreadsheets
- word processors
- DTP (desktop publishers).

Project management software

There are lots of different types of project management software available. Many of these can be used to create Gantt and PERT charts. The software may also be able to map the critical path.

One of the strengths of using project management software is that the tools required to, for example, link tasks or define milestones are built into the software. This makes the

Table 1.7 Strengths and weaknesses of planning tools

Planning tool	Strengths	Weaknesses
Gantt	Can show estimated time schedule Tasks are shown against a time schedule Comments can be added Resources for each task can be shown	Can be too simple for a complex project Task time is estimated so the plan may be unrealistic Task dependencies can be difficult to identify at the start of a project Not easy to identify critical path
PERT/Critical path	Can show slack time so resources can be reallocated Enables time scales to be planned Tasks can be scheduled as dependent or concurrent	Can become confusing Needs skill and knowledge to create Can be limited in large and complex projects
Visualisation diagram	Information and data can be understood quickly Emerging trends and patterns can be spotted quickly Non-specialists can understand the data/numbers being shown	Not appropriate for large and complex projects
Flow chart	Can be useful for simple projects with a small number of tasks and decisions Does not need any specialist project planning knowledge to understand the flow chart	Does not show time allocated for each task Tasks shown sequentially so does not show concurrent tasks
Mind map	Easy to add ideas/tasks at any time Can help focus on the tasks and links between them Shows dependent tasks	No time schedule Can be difficult for others to understand Does not show concurrent tasks
Task list	Can help focus on the tasks to be completed No tasks will be missed out	Should not be used for large and complex projects

creation of the project plan easier for the project manager and will enable them to create a complete and detailed project plan.

Table 1.8 Additional strengths and weaknesses of using project management software

Strengths	Weaknesses
Real-time changes can be made	Some project planning software is very expensive
Project plans can be shared electronically	There is a possibility that a simple project can become very complicated
Project plans can include allocated resources	Can be time consuming to set up a project
Reports can be generated to, for example, show the resources needed to complete each task	May need some knowledge/training/experience to use the software

Spreadsheets

Spreadsheets are designed to store and manipulate numbers, using functions and formulas. They are not designed to store files, annotations or any communication and collaboration. All of these things are essential to make a project successful.

However, if a Gantt chart is to be created, then it is possible to use a spreadsheet. Some spreadsheet software includes a template for a simple Gantt chart.

If a template is not available then it may only be possible to create a simple Gantt chart from scratch. Spreadsheets do not allow comments and audit trails to be created and seen by all members of the project team.

A spreadsheet could, however, be used to create a task list. The tasks could be defined down the left-hand side, with the projected start and end dates defined in the next columns.

A formula could then be used to calculate the number of days allocated to each task and the total number of days the project would take.

Word processors

Word-processing software can be used to create a range of informal plans including a task list or mind map. There are also in-built tools and features in word-processing software which allow shapes and lines to be used to create a flow chart.

DTP

DTP stands for desktop publishing software. This software can be used to create a visualisation diagram where images and text are combined.

DTP software can also be used to create a mind map or spider diagram.

One advantage of using DTP to create a plan is that the software allows different components from different files to be combined.

This means that images can be imported from, for example, a scanner or a graphics package. Text can be added from a word-processing file or inputted directly. The different components can be grouped, which means that a group of components can be moved as one.

 Activity

Investigate the different types of planning tools that could be created by different types of software. Fill in the table below to show which types of plans can be created by each type of software.

You may need to add more rows to the table.

Project management	Spreadsheet	Word processing	DTP

Top tip

You will need to select and use software during the planning phase of your coursework for R013. It is important that you select and use the most appropriate software to create the plans.

Practice questions

1   Describe **one** strength and **one** weakness of using project planning software to create project plans.   [4 marks]

2   Explain how spreadsheet software could be used to create a Gantt chart.   [3 marks]

LO2 To be able to initiate and plan a solution to meet an identified need

About this chapter

A project must be initialised and planned correctly from the beginning otherwise it will not be effectively carried out to completion. With careful planning and the selection and choice of the appropriate tools and techniques, a project will be more likely to go well and reach a successful conclusion so that the client gets what was set out in the client brief.

Tools and techniques should be carefully selected and used to ensure that the requirements set out in the client brief are met. The choices of the tools and techniques that you should use will depend upon the project that is being undertaken.

Choosing the correct tools and techniques ensures that a project is properly initialised and planned. A detailed project plan is very important as it sets out what has to be done, how it has to be done, how long the tasks in the project should take and when the project should be finished.

A well-planned project will enable the production of a technological solution for R013 to be completed successfully. The final product will be the technological solution that the client has asked for in the client brief.

Chapter content

2.1 How to initiate a project by analysing the requirements in a given context

2.2 How to mitigate risks through the planning process

2.3 How to create and use planning documentation

2.4 How to undertake iterative testing

2.1 How to initiate a project by analysing the requirements in a given context

All projects must be carefully planned. The first step in planning is to analyse the requirements of the client as set out in the client brief. The client brief will be developed and finalised during the initiation and the scene set for the project to proceed.

Key-word analysis

Analysing the key words in the **client brief** or list of requirements is important because these words highlight precisely what the client wants. This will allow you concentrate on planning exactly what needs to be done. Selecting the vital points in the brief is vital for proper planning so it is vital to make a good choice of relevant key words or aspects to pick out of the brief.

The first step in a **key-word analysis** is to read through the client brief and pick out the key words. For example, if a client wishes you to design a range of cakes suitable for sale in a tea shop, a search for words such as 'ingredients', 'presentation', 'costs' and 'food allergies' would highlight areas that must be considered when planning.

Study the list of key words and consider the relevance of each one; only words deemed to be important should be kept.

At this stage, other key words can be added by 'brainstorming'. For example, the cost of time and fuel to make the cakes may not be mentioned in the client brief, but could be important.

Research each key word, such as 'ingredients' or 'costs', to find out as much as possible about what it means or what needs to be done about it. For example, you might need to analyse the cost of ingredients in a spreadsheet, so a suitable spreadsheet would need to be designed and set up. Food allergies would need to be researched to ensure that customers are made aware of what ingredients are being used and where to ask for information about them.

Ranking the key words in order of importance enables you to make decisions when planning the project.

It may also be necessary to consider the hardware and software to be used, so you should analyse the brief to determine what is required, or what is already in place.

Key terms

Client brief The document that details the client's requirements.

Key-word analysis Analysing the client brief to determine and highlight the important aspects of the project.

SWOT analysis

SWOT analysis is used to identify the factors that will help or hinder the project. A SWOT analysis can be carried out by making a chart with four boxes, or using four pieces of paper, one each for Strengths, Weaknesses, Opportunities and Threats.

Table 2.1 SWOT analysis

Strengths These are factors that will help the project along.	**W**eaknesses These are factors that will slow the project down.
Opportunities These are factors that can be exploited to help the project along.	**T**hreats These are factors that could cause trouble or difficulties during the project.

Key term

SWOT Analysis to find out the Strengths, Weaknesses, Opportunities and Threats of/to a project.

For each, you must ask – and get good answers to – questions that will help ensure you are aware of factors that affect your ability to achieve a good outcome for the project. If the 'threat' questions that you ask (e.g. Is the project too expensive? Can I do this task? Is there enough time left?) have unfavourable answers then you must consider whether or not the project can be carried out.

SMART objectives

When the aspects of the project have been examined, the next step is to set **goals** and **objectives** for the project.

Key terms

Goal What you wish to be able to do.
Objective What you actually have to do or carry out.

You should create SMART goals and objectives:

Be **S**pecific: Clearly state or explain your objectives so that questions such as 'How many?', 'How can I tell when I have achieved this objective?' or 'How much will it cost to do this?' can be asked. Being specific enables you to tell when the objective has been met, so that it becomes measurable. An objective such as 'I will create a test plan' is completed when the answer to the question 'Have I created a test plan?' is 'Yes'.

Make **M**easurable objectives: You must be able to show that you have achieved an objective, so you should keep good records of what you have done and produce evidence to support it. A test plan, for example, can be evidence that an objective to create a test plan has been met and a question about its completion is answered with a 'Yes'.

The tasks and activities in the project must be possible. **A**chievable tasks are those that can be completed, for example a test plan is achievable because it can be created. It is important that you set yourself tasks that you can actually do, so be **R**ealistic and be sure that you are able to create a test plan, for example. If you are not realistic and you are unable to carry out the task or activity, then your project will fail. The **T**imes when the tasks or activities are due to be completed must be clearly stated, for example

'I will create a test plan by Monday.' The times must be sensible and achievable so that the project produces what the client wants, when it is wanted.

Project scope

All but very small projects must be broken down into manageable tasks so that activities can be given to different people. This allows a project to be completed faster than if one person does it all, and allows tasks to be carried out by people with specialised skills. Breaking a project down in this way is called 'scoping'.

Key term

Project scope Breaking down a project into manageable tasks.

Scoping can be done in various ways.

- Creating a task for every objective – e.g. to create a test plan – is a good method because it makes it easy to check what has been achieved so far.
- Creating a task for every job to be done – e.g. test a product – means that the whole job of creating a test plan, deciding on the tests, carrying out the tests and so on, becomes one task. This is good for very small jobs that do not really need to be broken into small steps.
- Creating a task for each day that you work on a project – e.g. 'On Monday, I will make a list of the tests to go in my test plan.' – can work well for long, complicated sets of tasks as it may give a sense of achievement at the end of each day.

Once the tasks are decided, a list should be made of them all. The activities that are necessary to complete each task can then be determined, i.e. 'I have to do *this activity* to complete *this task*.' An example of an activity would be 'To draw a table on paper' or, for the task of creating a test plan, 'To make a list of the tests to be carried out.'

Activity

You have been asked to create an advertising poster for a school open evening. You need some suitable images and some quotes from students to include in the poster. List the activities, in the order of when they should be done, that you should carry out when gathering the images and quotes and when getting them ready for inclusion in the poster.

Schedule

Tasks and activities

A task is something that must be done or completed. An activity is the action of doing the task. When the tasks and activities have been decided, a project schedule can be created. The tasks must be carefully examined to find out:

- how much time they will take
- who (if more than one person is involved in the project) is best suited to carry out each task
- what resources are needed for each task
- what other task(s) each task relies upon or leads to
- what contingencies must be allowed for.

Each task then has to be examined to decide the dependencies, so you need to decide which tasks or activities:

- can be done while other tasks are also being done? These are the concurrent or parallel tasks.
- have to be done first, before other tasks can start? These are sequential tasks.
- can start only after other tasks are completed? These are also sequential tasks.

Workflow

Workflow is the sequence of tasks, activities and processes that take place from the start of project through to its completion.

Timescales

Each activity in your project should have a time allocated to it. This will show how long it will take to complete each task. The time allocated should be sensible, so that the activity is not rushed but does not take too long. Once the timescales for the activities have been decided, you can create a **Gantt chart** and set milestones.

Activity

You have been set a task to draw a flower on a clean whiteboard and tell the class about the flower. It has to have a black outline with yellow petals and green leaves. Here is a list of activities that you have to carry out to complete the task.

- Talk to the class about the flower.
- Use a yellow pen to colour the petals.
- Use a green pen to colour the leaves.
- Erase the writing that was left on the whiteboard by the last user.
- Use a black pen to draw the outline.
- Pick up black, yellow and green pens.

Which tasks are sequential?

Which tasks can be carried out concurrently?

Remember to allow some extra time – but not too much – for solving problems, checking your work, and testing. Somewhere between 10 and 20 per cent more time should be enough to add to each activity. Some activities will need more than others; it is up to you to set a sensible amount of time for them. Managing your time is one of the most important aspects of carrying out your project.

Resources

Allocating and managing resources is vital to the success of a project. You must allocate time to activities, decide who is going to do which activity, when the activity needs to be done, why and where it is to be carried out, and what hardware and software will be needed for it. Making lists and documenting what resources you need and your allocation of resources will help to ensure that your project goes smoothly without any problems.

Milestones

A **milestone** is an important point in the timeline of a project. The start and end are important milestones, but other milestones may be when certain tasks have been completed; for example, the test plan has been completed. It's important that milestones do not slow a project down and are used only at important points.

Success criteria are needed so you can judge how well – or if – the objectives have been achieved and milestones have been reached. It is also important that you can justify why you have chosen your success criteria.

Contingency

Contingency enables the workflow and timescales to be planned and mapped out, along with the milestones that have to be reached. Contingencies can also be worked out, for example to allow for tasks to take longer than originally planned. Sometimes a task proves more difficult to do or takes longer because some resources are missing or some new skill has to be learned, so it is important to allow time for this to happen. You should try and work out the shortest and longest time it will take you to do each task or activity and then allow a little extra in case things go wrong. Do not allow too much contingency time as this will make a project far too long.

Links to other sections

You learned about workflow, contingency and milestones in Chapter 1, Section 1.1.

2.2 How to mitigate risks through the planning process

All projects carry the **risk** of not being completed on time, or even of not being completed at all. Good planning can reduce these risks.

The first step in **risk mitigation** is to admit that there are, or will be, risks. It is then possible to determine what the risks or threats are.

 Key terms

Risk A possible action or inaction to/in the project that slows it down or prevents it being completed.

Risk mitigation Creating options and actions to reduce risks and threats to the project.

Time

Often the most serious threat to a project is time – or a lack of sufficient time. A project only has a set amount of time to be completed because this is stated in the requirements document or client brief. Any action, or inaction, that causes a project to go beyond the set time is a threat to its successful completion. To try and avoid running out of time, activities and tasks must have an amount of time added to the estimated time to allow for problems to be solved. Often an extra 20 per cent is added as a contingency against unexpected problems.

Creating milestones at suitable points really helps with time management. It is clear when a milestone is or is not reached on time. If it is not, then action can be taken to speed up the activity.

Resources

It important that all hardware and software that will be used in the project are chosen carefully so that they comply with any regulations affecting their use and enable data to be kept safely and securely.

Legal

Laws and regulations that apply to the gathering and storing of data must be respected and followed. The provisions of the Data Protection Act 1998 and Computer Misuse Act 1988 require data to be kept safe and secure and not misused.

Links to other sections

You will learn more about the Data Protection Act 1998 and Computer Misuse Act 1988 in Chapter 4, Section 4.5.

Security

Security measures must be put in place to ensure that data is not accessed, edited or viewed by unauthorised persons, or lost or stolen. **Strong passwords** should be used because these can slow down or stop unauthorised access to your data. Weak **passwords**, dictionary words, or words relating to your personal details, such as names of pets, can be guessed or attacked with software that will try different words from a dictionary until it gains access.

Key terms

Password A set of characters that allows access to a computer system.

Strong password A password usually consisting of six or more characters that are a mixture of upper- and lower-case letters, numbers and symbols so that it is very difficult to guess. Not all computer systems allow all characters to be used.

Ethical and moral

Data must not be used for anything other than the purpose for which it was collected. Proper use of the data will avoid the risk of others accusing you of **bias** in how you've used the data or of **defamation of character**, even though you may not have intended it. It is also important to respect the privacy of the people from or about whom data is collected.

Key terms

Bias An unfair inclination towards or against a person or group of people.

Defamation of character Making a false statement about someone that causes them harm.

2.3 How to create and use planning documentation

Project planning software

Specialised software is used for project planning. With this software, tasks, activities, timescales and milestones can be set up. Tools for listing the tasks and their duration are provided. The software will then automatically create charts, as shown in Figure 2.1.

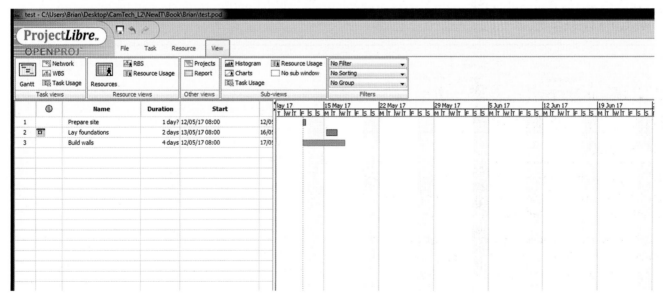

Figure 2.1 Creating a Gantt chart in Project Libre from the tasks entered on the left

Planning software also has a calendar to show available time slots and times when work cannot be done, as shown in Figure 2.2.

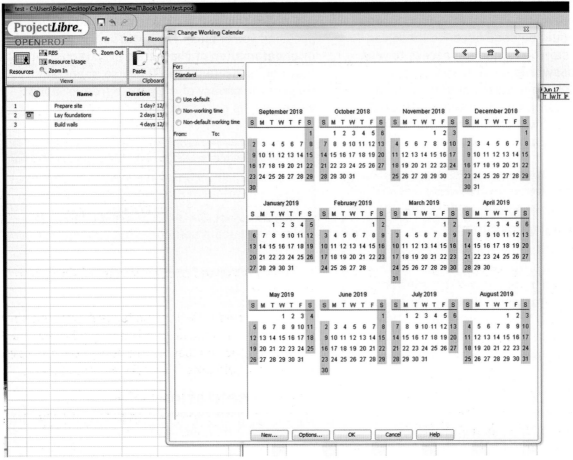

Figure 2.2 Calendar to show available time slots and times when work cannot be done

Project planning software includes tools for scheduling tasks, assigning resources to tasks and costing tasks, as well as being able to create charts and calculate critical paths. Reports can be exported as shown in Figure 2.3.

		Name	Duration	Start	Finish	Predecessors	Resource Names	Tue 9 May		
1		Prepare site	1 day?	12/05/17 08:00	12/05/17 17:00					
2		Lay foundations	2 days	13/05/17 08:00	16/05/17 17:00					
3		Build walls	4 days	12/05/17 08:00	17/05/17 17:00					

Figure 2.3 A report produced for the project in Figure 2.1

Reports can be used to provide an overview of the project, show up any risks early in the project, provide evidence to clients that the project is progressing, and give information on remaining tasks. Reports can also be used to alter workloads when workers are absent from work.

Spreadsheets

Spreadsheets are used in project planning. A good use for a spreadsheet is to calculate costs for each task and subtask.

| | Labour | | Materials | | | | | | | | BALANCE |
	HR	£/HR	UNIT	£/UNIT	TRAVEL	EQUIP/SPACE	FIXED	MISC	BUDGET	ACTUAL	UNDER/OVER
Project									£600.00	£1,590.00	-£990.00
Task	8.0	£30.00	100.0	£5.00			£50.00		200.00	790.00	-590.00
Task	8.0	£15.00			30.0		£100.00		300.00	250.00	50.00
Task			50.0	£11.00					100.00	550.00	-450.00
SubTask									-	-	-
SubTask									-	-	-
SubTask									-	-	-
SubTask									-	-	-
Task									-	-	-
Task									-	-	-
SUBTOTAL		£45.00		£16.00	30.0		£150.00	0.0	600.00	£1,590.00	-990.00

Figure 2.4 A spreadsheet for calculating costs for each task and subtask

Spreadsheets can require skill to set up properly. They can also be hard to read if there is lots of data as zooming loses the overview, and can be difficult to print to show others. Nonetheless, they are very powerful tools for specific tasks. Spreadsheets are very good for managing costs, tracking the progress of tasks and activities, providing data for reports and for tracking risks and threats. They are not, however, as good as specialised software for managing teams of people doing different activities, or for producing Gantt charts or collaborating with others on a project. If you use a spreadsheet to create a Gantt chart or to collaborate with others during your project, keep records of how easy it was – or not – so that you can include your views in your evaluation.

Project planning tools

Gantt charts and Critical Path

Identified tasks and activities should be placed into a flow chart and a **PERT** chart to visualise the project. The data from these charts can be used to create a Gantt chart or a network diagram in order to calculate how long the project will take from start to completion. These show concurrent (parallel) tasks and sequential tasks, along with their timings.

Table 2.2 shows a list of some tasks that would be carried out when making and serving a breakfast of scrambled eggs on toast with a cup of tea, and how long each would take. The tasks are not in order.

Table 2.2 Task list for making breakfast

Task	Time taken
Boil kettle of water	5 mins
Cook the eggs in a pan	3 mins
Crack two eggs into a bowl and scramble them	1 min
Gather ingredients ready to make breakfast	1 min
Pour hot water into tea cup and make tea	1 min
Put butter on the toast	1 min
Put scrambled egg on to the toast	1 min
Serve to table	2 mins
Slice bread	1 min
Toast the bread	3 mins

Each of the tasks must follow at least one of the other tasks otherwise the breakfast would not be made properly. In Table 2.3 each task is examined to deduce the correct order.

Table 2.3 Putting the tasks in order

Task no.	Task	Time taken for task (minutes)	Task must follow
1	Boil kettle of water	5	4
2	Cook the eggs in a pan	3	3
3	Crack two eggs into a bowl and scramble them	1	4
4	Gather ingredients ready to make breakfast	1	None
5	Pour hot water into tea cup and make tea	1	1
6	Put butter on the toast	1	10
7	Put scrambled egg on to the toast	1	6
8	Serve to table	2	5 and 7
9	Slice bread	1	4
10	Toast the bread	3	9

Key term

Critical path method A planning technique that aims to prevent time bottlenecks by showing the critical and non-critical tasks for the completion of a project

Activity

You have been asked to make some sandwiches with two fillings of your choice and serve them with a fizzy drink that has ice added. Write a list of tasks, and how long each would take, to prepare and serve the sandwiches and drink. Use planning tools to work out the sequential and concurrent tasks critical path.

Some tasks in this project can be carried out at the same time as other tasks. In this example, the eggs can be scrambled and the toast and tea can be made concurrently. Some tasks cannot be done at the same time – the tea can only be made after the water has been boiled. A Gantt chart can be created to show this. The shortest time for making and serving the breakfast can also be worked out.

Figure 2.5 is a Gantt chart made from Table 2.3, showing the shortest path through the whole project, covering all of the tasks. This path is called the critical path. Creating and using critical paths in project planning is called the **critical path method** or critical path analysis. The arrows show the critical path for this project, which is 9 minutes.

Project documentation

Data dictionary

For a spreadsheet

A project will often require the collecting, importing, storing and manipulating of data in a spreadsheet. The structure and format of the storage and the methods of manipulation must be defined before the spreadsheet is constructed and filled with data.

A **data dictionary** is used to plan out the spreadsheet for the project. A separate spreadsheet can be used to create a data dictionary.

Key term

Data dictionary A description of the structure, contents and format of a spreadsheet or database. The relationships within the database are also included.

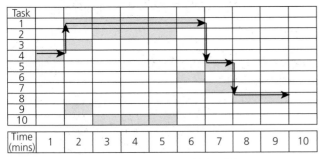

Figure 2.5 A Gantt chart made from Table 2.3

Figure 2.6 is an example of a simple data dictionary for a spreadsheet that works out the total cost of a journey to school with a visit to a shop on the way. It shows what is to be included, what sort of data is to be used and where the data is to be placed.

My Data Dictionary					
		Name of item	Type of data	Location of data	
		Bus fare	Text	B5	
		Drink	Text	B6	
		Snack	Text	B7	
		Magazine	Text	B8	
		Number bought	Numbers	C5 to C8	
		Cost of each item	Numbers	D5 to D8	
		Total cost	Calculated	D9	

Figure 2.6 A simple data dictionary for a spreadsheet

For a database

A data dictionary for a database contains all the information about the structure of the database. A data dictionary will have tables of information that list:

- the tables and their names
- the fields and their names
- the format and data types
- the relationships between the tables
- the validation rules
- the primary and other keys
- any other information needed to describe the database.

Key	Field name	Displayed title of field	Data type	Field size	Validation
Primary	student_ID		Autonumber		
	student_name	First name	Text	20	Presence
	student_family_name	Family name	Text	20	Presence
Foreign	class_teacher_ID	Class teacher	Integer		
	no_of_siblings	Siblings	Integer		Range

Figure 2.7 Part of a simple data dictionary for a database of school students

Visualisation diagrams

Visualisation diagrams show how a screen might look. They communicate ideas using images and help to focus and direct thoughts when producing designs.

Visualisation can be used to quickly show the costs of a product. Table 2.4 and Figure 2.8 show the costs of making a wooden chair as a list and as a pie chart. The pie chart is easier to take in quickly to see what costs the most or least.

Table 2.4 The costs of making a wooden chair as a list

Item	Cost (£)
Wood	25
Labour	30
Screws/nails	10
Paint	20
Seat cover	15

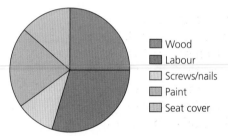

Figure 2.8 The costs of making a wooden chair as a pie chart

Diagrams can help visualise a project by showing the milestones, tasks and activities that are needed. Figure 2.9 shows a PERT chart for the preparing and serving of a simple breakfast, clearly showing which activities need to be carried out and in what order.

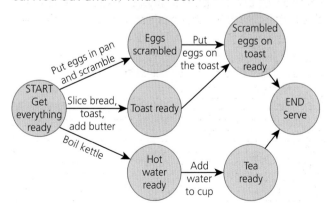

Figure 2.9 PERT chart for preparing and serving a simple breakfast

Timings can be added and the critical path can be determined. The critical path is shown in red in Figure 2.10.

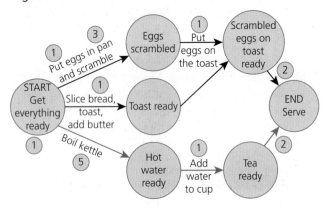

Figure 2.10 PERT chart for preparing and serving a simple breakfast, showing the critical path

Activity

How long is the critical path shown in Figure 2.10?

Asset logs

Asset logs are lists that show all the physical resources that will be used in a project. Resources include the hardware that will be used, software applications, templates and files, and drawings. The log should also show where the 'asset' can be found or used and where the files are stored. An asset log will allow you find the resources you need for a task.

Key term

Asset log A list of all the resources used in a project.

Activity

You have been asked to create a leaflet to advertise a school play. Make an asset log – including hardware and software – of what you need to make the leaflet ready for handing out.

Wireframes

A wireframe is a blueprint for a screen or a page. Wireframes show the proposed layout of the elements that will make up a screen or page.

A wireframe shows what the page or screen does and how the elements work together. Wireframes can be sketches done as early designs or they can be made in computer software. The benefit of having them in computer software is that they can be edited, shared and saved – they also look better. Wireframes can be used to help set house styles.

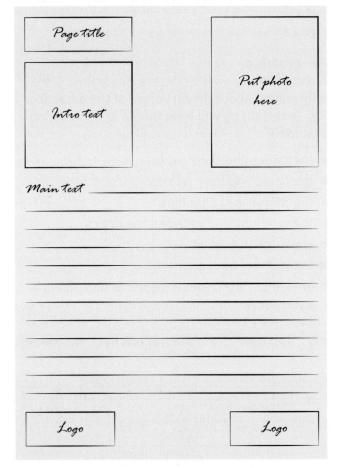

Figure 2.11 A hand-sketched wireframe

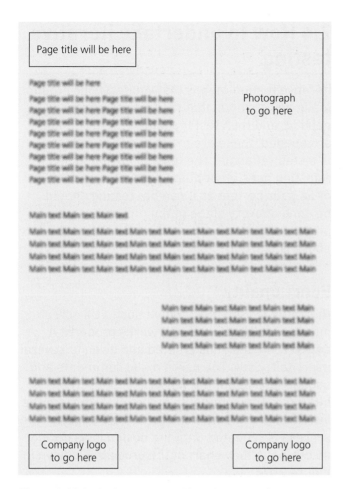

Figure 2.12 A wireframe created in computer software

Mock-ups of designs

A mock-up is a model of a design and is the next stage after the wireframe. It may or may not have working parts or some functionality. It is used for demonstration or design evaluation to see if the final product is likely to work or be acceptable to an end user. The end user may be the client who asked for the product to be designed and made, so the mock-up may be used to show the client how the final product might work.

A mock-up should:

● look as realistic as possible
● show which components go where
● have careful attention to detail
● be easily readable
● be flexible so that things can be changed.

A mock-up should not:

● be difficult to understand
● be cluttered with unnecessary items or elements that you think might be nice to have
● have too many colours and effects that obscure the purpose of the mock-up.

A mock-up of a screen layout can be produced on paper but will look much better if it is created in a software application. Digital versions of mock-ups can be easily scaled and amended immediately so a client can see any changes straightaway. Specialised software exists with design tools for creating mock-ups, but some designs can be done in graphics software. A typical design screen with tools is shown in Figure 2.11.

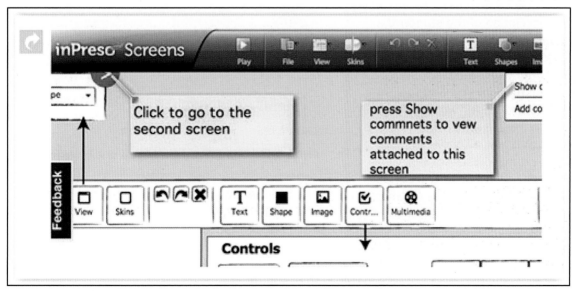

Figure 2.13 A typical design screen with tools

Prototype

A prototype is a close representation of the final product. Prototypes are essential when a user is testing your product. It is not essential for prototypes to look much like the final product, but those that are very similar to the final product do allow a better simulation of the interaction between users and the user interface.

Users can gain experience of the interface of the product by using a prototype and can test its functionality more easily. This means that users are better able to make comments and suggest improvements.

When to use wireframes, mock-ups and prototypes

Wireframes are useful in the beginning to quickly show what a user interface might look like, while mock-ups add more detail and can set **house styles**, colours, fonts and placing of images. Prototypes are working products that can be used for testing.

When designing a product, sketches can quickly create wireframes that share and organise your ideas. Wireframes can be used to design your mock-ups, which allow you to visualise and show the functionality of your product. When the mock-ups have been finalised, they are used as the basis for a working prototype.

Key term

House style A description of the standards for text and graphics in all of the documents to be produced or used by a company. A house style document sets out the colours that must be used, the font size and font style. It also lays out rules for where logos should go, how addresses and contact details should be shown and how all the text should be displayed, for example whether text should be left, right, centre or fully justified. A house style document makes sure that all the documents that come from the company look the same in layout and appearance so that customers can identify the documents as coming from the company.

2.4 How to undertake iterative testing

Iterative testing means that you test your product, make any changes that the tests show are needed, and then test it again. If more changes are needed, these are made and the product is tested yet again. The testing, changing and retesting goes on until the product is perfect, or as near perfect as it can be. Testing should be done at every stage of the project, with every product or part of a product tested before the next phase is started.

Functionality

Repeated testing of a product such as a screen interface will ensure that it works properly. A new screen design is created and given to several users to try out. The users make comments and suggestions about the working of the screen interface. The comments are used to improve the interface and the new design is tested again. This process is repeated until the design is as perfect as can be. A flow chart of the process is shown in Figure 2.14.

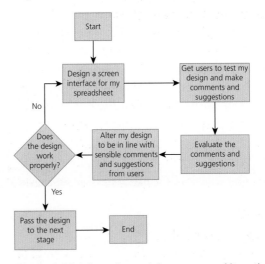

Figure 2.14 A flow chart of the process of iterative testing

The functionality of all the parts of the product and all aspects of the project must be tested and retested. Spreadsheets, databases, mail merges and all other components must be tested iteratively to make sure that they work as well as they should.

Usability

A product must be tested to see how easy it is to use. Real users or clients are asked to test out a product and report on how easy they find it to use. Their comments and suggestions are looked at and, if they are sensible and appropriate, changes to the product are made. Usability testing often compares one product with another to see if one works better than the other, or to show up what is missing from a new product, as well to highlight features that are not needed. Usability testing is another **iterative process** to ensure that the product is as good as it can be.

Key term

iterative process A process of repeatedly carrying out a process. Once the process is completed and the result is known or changes have been made, it is carried out again and the results are refined or more changes are made. This is repeated until no more changes are needed.

Accessibility

Products must allow 'non-standard' users to be able to use them. A screen interface must be accessible to people who have disabilities. The product must keep its functionality while doing this. A good product should cater for all people.

Top tip

To achieve high marks in the Evaluation section of R013 you must use iteration on all the phases of your project.

Test plans

Test plans are essential in making sure your product works properly. Every part and aspect of your product must be thoroughly tested. A client will not accept a faulty product and you will not achieve good marks in R013 if your product does not work or behave as it should.

Before writing a test plan, make sure you know what laws and regulations your product must comply with and include references to these with your plan.

A good test plan includes:

- the overall purpose of the tests
- what you will be testing and what you will not – there is no need to test well-known features of standard software but you should test how you use them to make sure they work in your product (there is no need to test features in software that you are not using)
- the data that will be used to carry out the tests and what you expect from using the data in the tests
- what resources are needed to complete the tests – the hardware and software requirements
- who will be doing the testing – you or other users?
- how and when you, or others, will be carrying out the tests – tests should be carried out as each part of a project and solution is completed and not just at the very end, when it may be too late to correct any errors or change things
- pass or fail criteria – so you know when a test is over or when it is time to give up on it
- how and when you will conduct retests when the tests show up errors or failures
- documents that accurately record the results of each test by each user.

Your test plan and the documents that record the tests can be used as evidence that you have tested your product at every stage. It should be used as part of the review in the evaluation stage of R013 to indicate what works well and what does not work quite so well, and what you have done about aspects that do not work as expected.

Types of data to use in testing

Testing of a software solution that requires data to be input and processed should use all the possible data that could be entered, as well as some data that the software should reject or that should cause errors. This is to find out how the software solution deals with the data. A well-designed solution will produce error messages for unacceptable data and deal with the data without failing.

Testing with **normal**, **extreme** and **erroneous data** is important so that the product will work properly when users input data.

An outline test plan is shown in Figure 2.15.

Key terms

Normal data Data that is acceptable to a computer system.

Erroneous data Data that is not acceptable to a computer system.

Extreme data Data that is on the boundary between data that is acceptable and data that is not acceptable to a computer system. Extreme data should be accepted by a computer system as it is still valid data.

Links to other sections

The IFERROR function may be useful when testing a product and considering how it will deal with errors. You will learn about this in Chapter 5, Section 5.1.

Top tip

Don't leave testing until the end of the project. Test each part of the process or each stage as you go along. Test the product as it is created. Keep detailed and accurate records of each test.

Testing of ....
Date of test ....

Test no.	Name of person doing the test	What is to be tested	Test data	Type of test data	Expected result of test	Actual result of test	Pass or fail?	Action to be taken	No. of retest if needed
1									
2									
3									
4									
..									
..									
..									

Figure 2.15 An outline test plan

Activity

A system is designed to add any two numbers. It will allow only numbers from 1 to 100 to be input.

- State two normal numbers that could be used for testing.
- State two erroneous numbers that could be used for testing.
- State two extreme numbers that could be used for testing.

LO3 Understand how data and information can be collected, stored and used

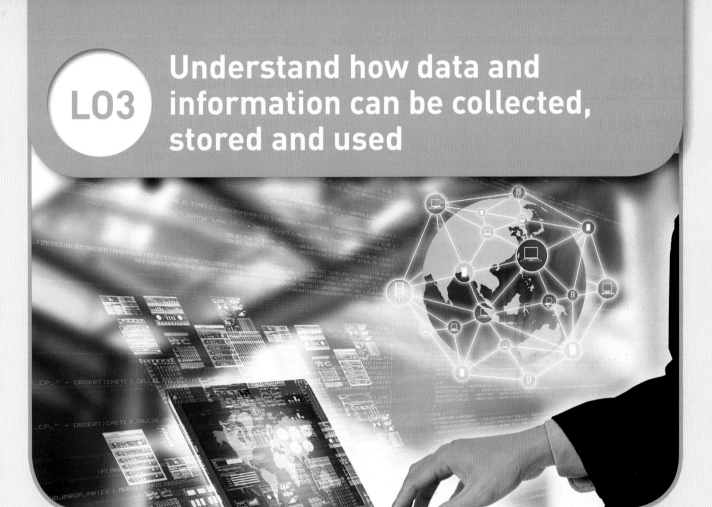

About this chapter

Computer systems can be used to collect, store and process data and information. In this chapter, you will learn about the difference between data and information. Many people confuse data and information, but it is important that you understand the difference between them.

Before data and information can be used, it needs to be collected and stored. You will learn about the different methods that can be used to collect data and information. Which method is used will depend on how the collected data and information will be stored, processed and used.

Data and information can have an impact on all parts of our lives. Once collected, data and information can be used in a range of applications, including education and shopping.

For data to be useful, it needs to be stored in a way that means it can be processed to produce useful results. This means that the type of data to be stored needs to be appropriate. There are many different data types; the selection of the data type can have an impact on how useful the data will be.

Chapter content

3.1 Data

What data is

Data is a big part of our lives. Lots of data is stored by government and businesses. But anything that is spoken or written down can also be classed as data. If you break down any words then you will find data.

 Key term

Data Raw facts and figures before they have been processed.

One definition is that 'Data is raw facts and figures before they have been processed.'

'Raw facts and figures' means they are without meaning; it is not possible to understand what the letters and figures mean.

Two examples of data are:

NAT23%7

56GHS56

It is not possible to know what these mean. They are just sets of random letters, numbers and symbols.

The main points about data are:

- Data has no meaning.
- Data is raw facts and figures before they have been processed.
- Data can be made up of letters, numbers, symbols, graphics and sound.

Data types and how they are used

Before data can be processed, the way in which it is to be stored must be considered. There are many different data types that can be used. Which type is chosen will depend on what data is to be stored and how it is to be processed. The data types that could be used include:

- text
- alphanumeric
- numeric (integer, real, currency, percentage, fraction, decimal)
- date/time
- limited choice (drop-down lists, **radio buttons**, tick lists)
- object
- logical/Boolean (yes/no, true/false).

Top tip

You should have learned about the different data types in your KS3 study.

When you are creating your project for R013 you will need to think about the data you will store and use. This will help you decide what data type you need to choose.

 Key term

Option boxes (or radio buttons) Allow users to select only one choice from two, mutually exclusive options. The choice is either 'this one' or 'that one', not both.

Table 3.1 gives details of all the different data types and how they are used.

Table 3.1 The different data types and how they could be used

Data type	Description	Example of data	How it could be used
Text	Any character	DB7&~?→hT5	To store names of items or people. Phone numbers are usually stored as text as this means they can have spaces and start with a 0
Alphanumeric	Any combination of letters, symbols, spaces or numbers	AjcY6&9£4	To store postcodes as these contain numbers and letters
Numeric types			
Integer	Whole numbers	1960	To store number of items in stock, number of lengths swum, number of tickets sold in one day to a live concert, TV channel number, years
Real	Any number, with or without decimal places	12.30	To store height/weight
Currency	Shows data in the format of money. It can be used to show currency signs (e.g. £ or $) and have decimal places to show the full currency details	£79.87	To store prices
Percentage	A number format that includes decimal places and a % sign	25%	To show a percentage of a discount, e.g. 25% off the price
Fraction	A number format, usually included in spreadsheet software, that enables actual fractions to be input and manipulated	$\frac{7}{8}$	To show the result of a calculation
Decimal	A number format that shows an exact number using a decimal point and numbers after the decimal point	22.75	To show the result of a calculation expressed as a decimal
Date/time	A date or time – there are different formats of date and time that can be used. Which one is chosen will depend on how the date/time is to be stored and processed	25/04/2017 19:15	To show a date, e.g. 25 April 2017, or a time, e.g. 19:15 or 7:15 p.m.
Limited choice	Restricts the choice by a user; can be used on an information-gathering document	A drop-down list, radio button, tick list	To select days of the week, or a radio button to select a payment method
Object	An additional component, usually found in a spreadsheet	A chart or graph taken from a different source	To insert a chart into a worksheet that has been taken from a different file
Logical/Boolean	There are only two choices, e.g. true or false	Yes or no, true or false, male or female, 1 or 0	To store the gender of a person, or to answer a closed question

Top tip

When you are creating your product for R013 you will need to define the data types you are going to use. You must make sure that the data types are appropriate and suitable for the types of data you are using and manipulating.

Activity

Fill in the table below to show how each data type could be used in the areas shown.

	School	Sports club	Shop
Real number			
Integer number			
Boolean			
Date/time			

3.2 Information

What information is

You have already learned that data on its own is meaningless. Information is created when data is processed.

The formula for converting data to information is:

Information = data + [structure] + [context] + meaning

Sometimes it is not necessary to give data structure and context for it to become information, but is it always better to know the full formula.

The *structure* of data is how it is presented. One example would be the structure for presenting dates. One way a date could be structured is 24/04/2017. The structure for this would be NN/NN/NNNN, where N shows that it should be a number.

Another example would be the structure for postcodes. The structure for a postcode would be LLNN NLL, where N is a number and L is a letter.

The *context* of data is what we need to know and understand to make sense of the data. For example, consider the data of:

15, cabbages, rabbits

This data means nothing. But when this data is put into a sentence, or context, the data makes sense:

15 cabbage plants were planted but the rabbits ate all of them.

The data now makes sense as a context has been provided.

The *meaning* of data is revealed when it is in the correct structure and put into context.

Table 3.2 How data, structure, context and meaning can be used to get information

Data	Structure	Context	Meaning
01012017	NN/NN/NNNN 01/01/2017	A UK date	New Year's Day in 2017
30 40 50 60 70	Integer numbers	Miles per hour	Speed limits on different types of UK roads and motorways
TRNB14	First two letters: type of clothing Second two letters: colour Last two numbers: UK size LLLLNN	A clothing shop stock code	A navy-blue pair of trousers, UK size 14

Activity

Fill in the table below to show how data can be turned into information. The first one has been done for you.

	Shoe shop	Sports club	School
Data	MTNSS10		
Structure	LLLLLNN		
Context	A shoe shop stock code		
Meaning	Men's trainers, non-slip soles, size 10		

How data and information are related

You have already learned about how information is:

data + [structure] + [context] + meaning

Data and information are related. This means that there are links between data and information. The main links you need to be aware of are that:

- information is in context, while data has no context
- information is data that has been coded/ structured
- data must be processed to become information.

Practice questions

1 Describe the difference between data and information. **[2 mark]**

2 Describe **one** characteristic of data. **[2 mark]**

3 Using an example of the stock number NBLT16, show how this data can be turned into information. **[4 mark]**

3.3 The methods used to collect data and store data/ information and the IT used to support data collection

The methods used to collect and store data/information

There are many different methods that can be used to collect data and information. The method that is chosen will depend on:

- what data and information is to be collected
- where the data and information is to be collected
- how the collected data and information will be stored and processed.

Questionnaires/surveys (online and hard copy)

A questionnaire/survey contains a set of questions that are designed to collect data and information from the people completing the questionnaire. A range of types of questions can be asked, including:

- **closed**
- **open**
- **rank order**
- **rating**.

Key terms

Closed question A question where there is only a set number of answers to be chosen, for example for 'Can you ride a bicycle?' the answers would be either 'Yes' or 'No'.

Open question Allows the person completing the questionnaire to give a detailed answer in their own words.

Rank order Requires the person completing the questionnaire to compare a list of the same type of items. The items are then ranked, for example from 1 to 10 where 1 is very important and 10 is least important.

Rating Requires the person completing the questionnaire to compare different items. The items are then ranked, for example from 1 to 10 where 1 is very important and 10 is least important.

A questionnaire must be created knowing how the data and information will be stored and processed. Questionnaires are an excellent way to collect statistical data and information. Rating and rank order questions can be very useful if statistical information is required, as all the answers will be numerical.

A questionnaire can be completed on paper and collected when complete. This method means that the data and information must be input into the software package before any processing can be carried out. This can often introduce errors.

Online questionnaires and surveys are technology-based. The questionnaire/survey can be provided by email, on a website or in the cloud. As each person completes and submits their answers, the data and information can be automatically input into the software used for the analysis. This method means there is less chance of errors in the data and information being stored and processed.

Activity

Create a questionnaire/survey to ask your classmates about what they use the internet for, when and for how long. You should use a range of different question types.

Find a free online survey tool and create an online questionnaire/survey from your questions.

Email

Information can be gathered using email. An email can be sent that includes an interactive form to be completed or a link to an online survey.

If the email contains an interactive form then the email has to be replied to. The form can then be completed and returned to the sender. It is possible for information gathered in this form to be imported into a spreadsheet or database.

The interactive form must be in the same structure as the spreadsheet or database and include the same fields. This allows the information to be inputted automatically into the software with little risk of human error.

If the email contains a link to an online form then the process is the same as that mentioned in the section above on questionnaires.

Sensors

A sensor is a device that responds to a change or input from the environment. Inputs for a sensor could include light, heat or motion. The output from the sensor is usually a signal that is converted to a human-readable display or transmitted electronically over a network for reading or further processing.

Sensors can be found in cars and wearable technology and as part of a connected house system. There are many different types of sensors, for instance motion sensors. The most common type of motion sensor is passive infrared (PIR). This works by detecting heat, for example, when someone walks past the PIR. This type of sensor can be used to switch outside lights on and off or to activate a burglar alarm. When these are used as part of the connected house, then, if a burglar alarm is activated, the data about this can be sent directly to the police or to a monitoring company.

Another type of sensor is a pressure sensor. These can be used to collect data by counting the number of times the sensor is activated by pressure, such as counting cars going along a road. Another example is a pressure pad sensor placed at the entrance to a museum to count the number of people entering.

Figure 3.1a A sensor recording traffic flow

Figure 3.1b A motion sensor in an outside light

If this type of sensor is to be used to count people, the location must be carefully chosen. There is a danger, if placed incorrectly, that people both entering and exiting the museum will be counted, which would lead to false data being collected.

A PIR sensor could also be used if the data is collected each time the infrared beam is broken. But, as with the pressure sensors, where this is placed must be carefully considered.

Activity

Investigate the range of sensors that can be used in the connected house. Describe the purpose of each sensor you find. Discuss your findings in a group.

Interviews

An interview is a conversation between two people in which questions are asked. For this reason, interviews are usually completed one to one, face to face. The questions to be asked need to be planned in advance, based on how the data and information collected will be processed. The **interviewer** asks questions of the **interviewee**.

Key terms

Interviewer The person asking the questions.

Interviewee The person answering the questions.

The type of questions asked will depend on the data and information that is to be collected and how it will be stored and processed. An interview will not usually contain rank or rating questions, but may contain some closed questions. Most of the questions will be open.

The data and information gathered during the interview will need to be manually input into the software being used to store and process it.

Consumer panels

A consumer panel is a group of people who are asked by a business to give their opinions and advice about products and services. The panel gives feedback about products and services through a series of questions.

If a product is to be tested, then the panel may be given the product to use before they provide their feedback. For example, if a new coffee machine has been developed, the manufacturer may provide a coffee machine to each person on the panel to use.

The panel could also be given initial designs, or a mock-up, of a new product. They will be able to provide feedback on how it looks and make suggestions about how it could be improved.

Much of the feedback given by a consumer panel will be each person's own opinions. But, if the panel is formed from people of different ages, occupations, etc. then the feedback given will be varied and helpful to the business.

The consumer panel may also be asked to provide feedback, for example on changes to a business's website or on a new TV advert before it goes out on air. These are called services. The feedback provided by the consumer panel could be completed in a face-to-face meeting or using an online questionnaire.

Activity

Think about one product and one service that a consumer panel could be asked to provide feedback on.

Develop some questions that could be answered by the panel to provide the feedback.

Loyalty schemes

Loyalty schemes seem to be everywhere. Every adult living in the UK will have at least one loyalty scheme card in their purse or wallet. Loyalty schemes are offered by a range of businesses. These can range from retailers to petrol and hotel chains.

A loyalty scheme is a rewards programme offered by a business to its customers. In return for belonging to the loyalty scheme, customers can earn points that can be converted into money-off vouchers for shopping or other rewards, such as days out to a tourist attraction or free hotel stays.

Activity

Investigate different loyalty schemes that are available. Try to find schemes that are run by different types of businesses.

If a customer belongs to a retailer's loyalty scheme, points are added to their loyalty card record when they shop at the retailer, both online and on the high street. The process of adding points to a customer's record would be:

- The customer record is located in the database.
- When payment has been accepted, the cost of the goods is converted to points.
- The new points are added to the current points total.
- The new points total is updated in the customer record.

The loyalty scheme may be used to give customers advanced access to new products, targeted money-off vouchers or free goods. The business running the loyalty scheme can use the loyalty scheme data to target offers to a customer. For example, if the customer record shows that they regularly buy dog food, money-off vouchers can be sent that relate to dog products.

With some retailers, at regular intervals, usually every three months, the points are converted into

Figure 3.2 Loyalty schemes

money-off vouchers. These vouchers are then posted or emailed to the customer.

Some loyalty schemes allow the customer to redeem their points when they want to. The customer can choose the item or service they want to exchange the points for. The number of points used is then subtracted from their points total.

Activity

Develop the steps that would take place when:
- a customer redeems points
- the business sends out money-off vouchers.

Statistical reports

A wide range of statistics that have already been collected can be found on the internet. These statistics can be analysed to provide further data and information.

Statistics can be found on many websites, but the validity of these should be confirmed before they are used. It is always best to find statistics on websites that can be trusted, for example, the websites of the different government departments.

One of the largest collections of statistics can be found from the census. The census takes place in the UK every 10 years and is completed by every household. The census is carried out by the Office for National Statistics (ONS), which also processes all the data.

There are many different datasets on the ONS website, such as the value of e-commerce sales. This dataset shows the increase in sales through e-commerce related to different areas, such as retail and hotels. There are also datasets that can be searched about your home or school area. There are also datasets which can be searched about your home or school area. One website that stores these datasets is www.streetcheck.co.uk. This website enables people to search for statistics based on a postcode. The categories of statistics that can be found include the population, types of housing and broadband speeds.

Activity

Access the Street Check website and look at the neighbourhood statistics for your local area using your postcode.

Try to analyse the statistics. Are they a good representation of your neighbourhood?

By looking at collected statistics it is possible to spot trends or patterns. For example, the website www.metoffice.gov.uk provides statistics on weather, including hours of sunshine and amount of rain, for the United Kingdom. By looking at these statistics, some of which have been processed into graphs, it is possible to see trends.

Activity

You have been asked to collect some statistics about the use of a shop from Monday morning until Friday evening when the shop closes.
- What data and information could you collect?
- How would you collect the data and information?
- What would be the format of the data you would collect?
- How could you process and present the data and information you have collected?

Secondary research methods

There are two different types of research methods: primary and secondary.

- A *primary* research method is where the data and information collected is fresh data collected for a specific purpose.
- *Secondary* research methods use data and information that has already been collected. A good example of secondary research is using a book to find out statistics that have already been collected and, possibly, processed.

The methods you have already learned about can be divided into primary and secondary, as shown in Table 3.3.

Table 3.3 Primary and secondary research methods

Primary	Secondary
Questionnaires	Statistical and trends/reports
Sensors	Loyalty schemes
Interviews	
Loyalty schemes	

You can see that loyalty schemes can provide both primary and secondary research. This is because the business running the loyalty scheme will collect the data (primary research). But, a manufacturer of a product may also use the data from the loyalty scheme to target marketing at customers based on their history of purchases (secondary research).

The main difference between primary and secondary research is the source of the data and information. There are also other differences between primary and secondary research, as shown in Table 3.4.

Table 3.4 Other differences between primary and secondary research

	Primary	Secondary
Meaning	Research that collects first-hand or fresh data for a specific purpose	Research that uses data and information that has already been collected
Based on	Raw data and information	Analysed and processed data and information
Carried out by	The researcher	Someone else
Data	Specific to the purpose	May not fully meet the specific needs
Process	Very involved	Quick and easy
Cost	High	Low
Time	Long	Short

There are advantages and disadvantages to each research method, as shown in Table 3.5. Which is chosen will depend on how the data and information is to be collected, stored and processed.

Table 3.5 Advantages and disadvantages of different methods of collecting data and information

Method	Advantages	Disadvantages
Questionnaires/ surveys	Large numbers of people can be asked to fill in the same questionnaire/survey Comparisons are easy to formulate (e.g. 75 per cent of people liked the new company logo) Cheaper than interviews for large numbers of people	If the questionnaire/survey is online, people need the technology to be able to complete it A badly designed question may not get the data required in the right format
Emails	The same email can be sent to many people at the same time The results from the emails can be automatically input into software for analysis/manipulation Little risk of human error occurring when the data collected is input into the software	Emails may be diverted into spam/junk folders by the email provider If the fields or data types are not exactly the same as the fields being used for analysis/manipulation then the data collected may be worthless
Sensors	Once set up, do not need human intervention as the data collected can be sent electronically The data collected by a sensor is usually more accurate than that taken by people, for example, people may lose count but sensors just keep working	The positioning of sensors needs to be carefully considered as incorrect placing could result in worthless data being collected Sensors may stop working, for example if there is a power cut
Interviews	Questions can be modified based on the answers given to previous questions A rapport can develop between the interviewer and the interviewee that may result in questions being answered honestly Additional questions can be asked to clarify any answers already given	Can be time consuming and costly to carry out Poor interviewing can lead to misleading or insufficient data and information being gathered Not suitable for gathering data and information from large numbers of people
Consumer panels	The cost of consumer panel feedback can be low if online feedback methods are used The feedback provided is specific to the product or service Response rates are high as members of the panel have agreed to take part	If products need to be provided to the panel, the cost may be high in terms of the actual product and the delivery to members of the panel If there isn't a range of people on the panel, the feedback could be biased towards one specific type of person The format of the feedback needs to match the processing that is to be carried out
Loyalty schemes	A loyalty scheme can help keep customers using the business The data collected each time a customer uses their loyalty card can provide information on the habits of the customer	Some people feel that the data collected about them through using a loyalty scheme can be an invasion of privacy
Statistical reports	If a trusted source is used, then the statistics are readily available, cover a range of topics and are reliable Some processing may have already been carried out Statistics can show trends and patterns that can help with decision making	May not have been collected for the same purpose so may not provide clear and full data Statistics need to be collected knowing how they are going to be analysed/processed and stored Statistics show data from a sample of people rather than a true representation
Secondary research methods	The data has already been collected and possibly processed Data collection is quicker than having to collect the data first-hand	The data may not be exactly what is required It is not always possible to tell if the data is real/ genuine

Activity

For each method, identify two collection activities where it could be used.

Discuss your findings with the rest of your class.

Practice questions

1 Compare the use of online and hard-copy surveys. **[4 marks]**

2 Describe **two** advantages and **one** disadvantage of the use of sensors to collect data about people entering a shop. **[6 marks]**

3 Explain how loyalty-scheme data could be used by manufacturers. **[4 marks]**

4 Discuss how statistical reports from a government website could be used when researching climate change. **[10 marks]**

Information technology used to support data collection

You have already learned about some methods that can be used to collect data and information. Some of these methods can be carried out using information technology (IT).

Barcode readers

Barcode readers are used to scan barcodes. Every product has a unique barcode that allows it to be identified and store data about the product. Barcodes can help retailers to identify products and to use the information for stock control.

Figure 3.3 A barcode

 Activity

Investigate the barcodes you can find in your school.

Barcodes can be linked with loyalty schemes. When a shopper goes into a supermarket, the products they buy are scanned at the till. These products will be linked through the barcodes to their unique loyalty scheme number. This allows the supermarket to identify which goods a shopper buys. This information can then be used to send targeted offers, discounts and money-off vouchers to shoppers.

Some supermarkets use a system called *shop and scan*. This is known by different names in different supermarkets, for instance Scan as you Shop (Tesco), Smart Shop (Sainsbury's) or Quick Check (Waitrose). This allows members of the loyalty scheme to scan their own products. When the shopper has finished, they go to a dedicated till where the data about their shopping is transferred to the till and linked to their loyalty scheme number. When the data transfer is complete the shopper pays for their shopping.

 **Activity**

Investigate the use of the shop-and-scan system.

Identify the advantages and disadvantages to the supermarket and the shopper of using this system.

QR codes

Quick Response (QR) codes are two-dimensional barcodes that store data.

Figure 3.4 A QR code

A QR code, as shown in Figure 3.4, is made up of black modules in a square pattern on a white background. A QR code can hold more data and be read more quickly than a standard bar code.

QR codes can be used in advertising, for instance in magazines or on posters. The codes can be read, or scanned, by a smartphone. The information held in the QR code can then be interpreted by the smartphone. This information could include a URL, a discount voucher, or the contact details of a business.

Activity

Find a range of QR codes for different businesses. Scan the QR codes to see the information contained in them.

Web-based surveys

Web-based surveys are surveys that are located on the internet. You learned about questionnaires and surveys earlier in this chapter. To access and complete a web-based survey, a device must be connected to the internet. This device could be a smartphone, tablet or computer. When the survey has been completed, the responses are submitted and are usually saved in a spreadsheet or database.

By using these types of software, the company carrying out the survey can store and process the submitted data.

Activity

Use the internet to find some web-based surveys. Look at the questions that are included and identify how the data collected could be used.

Wearable technology

Wearable technology refers to smart electronic devices that can be worn. Examples of wearable technology include activity trackers, smartwatches and headsets.

Wearable technology is a good example of the **internet of things**; for example, a fitness tracker could store fitness data in a file on the manufacturer's website. This would allow progress to be tracked and even compared with that of friends.

Key term

internet of things The interconnection via the internet of computing devices embedded in everyday objects, enabling them to send and receive data.

Activity

Investigate either fitness trackers or smartwatches. Develop a list of features that your device includes. Think about how your type of device could be used.

Another example of wearable technology is glasses. This is still quite a new technology. The glasses allow the wearer to view text notifications via a heads-up display on the lenses of the glasses. Apps can also be used with the glasses, for example to read newspaper articles.

Figure 3.5 Wearable technology

Mobile technologies

Mobile technology refers to any device that can be transported by the user. Examples of mobile technology include smartphones, tablets, GPS devices such as satnavs, and ebook readers. These devices provide the user with instant access to information via the internet.

The increased use of the cloud has made mobile technology even more popular, as it allows files and documents to be accessed 'on the move'.

Links to other sections

You will learn more about the cloud in Section 3.4 of this chapter.

Practice questions

1 Explain how retailers can use the data collected when the barcodes of products are scanned at a till. **[4 marks]**

2 Explain how wearable technology can help people keep track of their personal fitness. **[4 marks]**

3 Mobile technology can be used to gather information and data from the internet. Describe **one** advantage and **one** disadvantage of mobile technology. **[4 marks]**

Top tip

You will need to keep up to date with developments and emerging technology during your course.

3.4 Different storage methods and the appropriateness of the use of these in context

When data and information has been collected, it needs to be stored before it can be processed. You will need to know about the cloud and physical storage devices.

The cloud

The cloud has a very large storage capacity and is made up of a lot of servers that store and locate data and information. The cloud refers to software, services and storage areas that run on the internet rather than being stored and accessed on a physical storage device.

Cloud services and storage are accessed through a web browser, such as Mozilla Firefox or Google Chrome. An increasing number of cloud service providers also offer access through an app.

Cloud services include Dropbox, Microsoft OneDrive and Amazon Drive. Many people store files, including documents, pictures and videos, in the cloud. By doing this, the files can be accessed from anywhere as long as an internet connection is available.

Using the cloud to store and view large files – such as documents, photo collections and videos – means that the user requires less physical memory on their device, for example, their laptop, tablet or smartphone.

The cloud servers process and store the files, so users do not need to buy high-specification devices to access and work on the files. Many businesses use the cloud to enable collaborative working on files, which means that many employees can now work remotely and do not have to travel into an office.

The biggest problem with using the cloud to access and work on files is that it requires an internet connection. Without an internet connection, or with a slow/unstable connection, the files, software and apps stored in the cloud can be inaccessible. The files, software and apps are also inaccessible if the cloud servers stop working or 'go down'.

The other problem with storing files in the cloud is that of security. As the data and information 'lives' in the cloud, there is always a risk of it getting into the wrong hands if the storage space in the cloud is hacked. There are prevention measures that can be put in place, but it is wise to carefully consider what data and information is stored in the cloud.

Physical devices

The most common physical devices are shown in Table 3.6.

Links to other sections

You will learn more about prevention measures in Chapter 4, Section 4.4.

Table 3.6 The most common physical devices

Storage device	Features	Typical uses
Hard disk drive	A hard disk drive uses magnetic disks for storing software and data in files The disks are circular and spin at high speeds while drive heads read and write the data; this makes the disks susceptible to dirt and damage if moved suddenly The files can be read, edited, re-written or deleted Hard disks can store huge amounts of data	Storage of the operating system Storage of files and data not in use at the time Storage of data, files and software when the computer is turned off Storing a database of the details of members
Solid state drive	A solid state drive uses flash memory to store software and data in files There are no moving parts in solid state drives, which makes them faster and more reliable than magnetic hard disk drives They are often found in portable computers such as netbooks and tablet computers Solid state drives are faster in use than hard disks They can store as much data as a hard drive, but are much more expensive to buy	Storage of the operating system Storage of files and data not in use at the time Storage of data, files and software when the computer is turned off
Optical device	An optical drive uses optical media, such as CDs and DVDs, to store software and data in files The files can be read, edited, re-written or deleted only if CD-R/RWs or DVD-R/RWs are used Data stored on CD-ROMs and DVD-ROMs can be read but cannot be altered Blu-Ray Discs™ are large-capacity optical disks and can store very large amounts of data	Storage of files or data that have to be moved to another computer Storage software for installation on a computer Storage of data, files and software in backups or archives
Flash memory device	Small memory sticks contain flash memory and are used in USB ports They are used to store data and files for transfer to other computers, for taking to/from the office, in cameras and phones as the memory card	Save a file on to a memory stick (flash memory device) Save images in a camera Save contact details in a phone

Top tip

In your exam, you may need to be able to select and justify the storage devices to be used in a context. When you are completing your project for R013 you may need to select the storage devices you will use.

Practice questions

1 Describe **two** features of a USB memory stick that make it suitable for transferring files between computers. [4 marks]

2 Explain **two** reasons why a supermarket might decide to store files in the cloud rather than in its own file servers. [4 marks]

3 Explain the advantages to a team who are working remotely of uploading and using files in the cloud. [6 marks]

3.5 The use of data, the applications and interaction of data stores, and the benefits and drawbacks of the use of data

The amount of data that is being collected, processed and stored is growing every day. Big Data is the term given to these large data sets.

Big Data is data sets that are so big or complex that traditional data processing software cannot deal with them. Big Data is usually measured in terms of petabytes (1024 terabytes) or exabytes (1024 petabytes), so Big Data really is *big*!!

Big Data isn't just about how much data is collected and stored, but how it is processed. Data can be taken from any source and processed and analysed to find trends and patterns.

Big Data can be used in a range of applications. Little data stores can interact with Big Data stores. Big Data stores can also interact to form even bigger data stores.

Applications and interaction of data stores

Data can be used by many different areas or applications. You have already learned how data can be collected; in this section you will learn about how the stored data can be used.

Law enforcement

Law enforcement is one area that benefits from the use of data and Big Data. There are many ways that law enforcement can use data stores. For example, the police have a system called **ANPR** in some of their police cars.

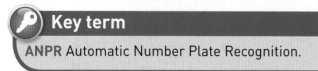

Key term

ANPR Automatic Number Plate Recognition.

This system checks the number plate of every vehicle that the police car sees. When a number plate is seen, the ANPR system can interact with

DVLA to check who owns the vehicle and whether they have a current driving licence. The system can also check if the car is taxed and, if required, if it has a current MOT.

These checks are done almost instantly as the vehicle passes the police car, and if there is a problem with the vehicle then an alert is displayed on the screen of the ANPR device. This alert will then prompt the police to stop the vehicle to talk to the driver.

Speed cameras, on motorways and roads, use a similar system. As a vehicle passes a speed camera, the camera takes a measurement of its speed. If the vehicle is travelling at or below the speed limit, then no action is taken. If the speed limit is being broken, however, the camera takes a picture of the number plate. The number plate is then looked up using the DVLA database and a speeding notice is sent to the registered owner of the vehicle.

Figure 3.6 Law enforcement using data stores: the ANPR system

Another example of the use of Big Data in law enforcement is the use of CCTV. CCTV cameras are a common sight. They are used to monitor what is happening in a street, shopping centre, railway station or airport. If anything suspicious is spotted on the video screen linked to the CCTV camera, the emergency services – police, fire or ambulance – can be called to deal with the problem.

Some CCTV cameras link to facial recognition systems that are held by the police and other security services. Facial recognition systems allow the security services to track people they feel are suspicious or whom they want to arrest.

The police have developed a Police National Database (PND) that allows all the police forces in the UK to share information about criminal activity. Each force inputs data, and is able to query data that has been entered by the other forces. The main aim of the PND is to enable police forces to share intelligence about criminals and illegal activities.

 Activity

In groups, investigate how Big Data is used in law enforcement, including the Police National Database. Present your findings to the class.

Education

There are many uses for data in education, for instance data collected by schools can be analysed to show how well students are doing and how much progress they are making.

 Activity

Investigate how progress data is collected in your school. Find out how it is collected, processed and analysed. How is it used to provide your targets and predicted grades in your Year 11 qualifications?

There are many other ways in which data can be used in education. Many colleges and universities offer Massive Open Online Courses (**MOOCs**). These courses collect the data and information entered by students as they complete the course. This data and information is then processed and analysed to provide students with a grade when they have completed the course. The data and information collected can also be used to make changes to the content of the course materials.

 Key term

MOOC A Massive Open Online Course is an online course with unlimited numbers of students and open access via a website.

Data can also be used by schools in different parts of the world. Schools can use data that has been collected, stored and processed to help with their students' studies. Data that is stored in the cloud can be accessed and downloaded. The data that is downloaded can then be used, for example, to complete coursework where it is not possible to use primary sources to collect the data.

 Activity

Research other ways in which data and information can be used in education. Present your findings in a report.

Health and fitness

Links to other sections

You learned about wearable technology in Section 3.3 of this chapter.

Wearable technology can be used to track the fitness progress of the person wearing the technology.

Research into disease and illness can also produce data. There are many different research teams based all over the world researching the same illness or disease, for example, cancer.

Research data collected by a number of research teams can be shared, usually through the cloud. This could enable a cure or better treatments to be found. Many diseases are being researched around the world by teams using Big Data that has been collected, stored and processed.

Some research teams are using apps to collect data. The apps require people with a specific disease to input their own readings, for example, blood glucose levels for diabetes. This allows data to be collected from a wider range of people than if the research team had to collect the data.

Activity

Use the Health section of the BBC website and other health-related websites (e.g. Cancer Research UK) to investigate the use of data collection for different diseases.

Shopping

Links to other sections

You learned about loyalty schemes in Section 3.3 of this chapter.

Retailers capture information and data every time a shopper uses their loyalty card. This data is stored and can then be processed to identify trends and patterns. The data of all the loyalty scheme members can be analysed, for example to identify how popular a particular product is.

Retailers can also use the data collected through loyalty schemes to identify which products should be on special offer.

Retailers can collect data at the tills or from online shopping baskets. This data does not depend on loyalty schemes but provides details of every product sold. This data can be used by manufacturers, for example to target marketing, advertising and special offers.

Entertainment and leisure

Big Data is collected each time a digital or satellite TV channel or a film/video is watched or music is streamed. Data is also collected when we go to the cinema to watch a new release film.

The entertainment industry is very competent at processing and analysing this data. Decisions concerning films made by big Hollywood studios are based on which films have made the most money at the box office or on streaming websites.

Decisions to make TV programmes are also based on viewing figures, both live and on catch-up media. For example, BBC TV programmes such as *Call the Midwife* have had consistently high viewing figures since the series was first shown. These viewing figures have meant that several series of the programme have been produced.

Film and TV producers can also see how popular box sets have been. These are a complete set of the programmes in a series, which can be downloaded and watched one after the other. For example, box sets of the *Game of Thrones* TV series have been one of the most popular downloads.

By gathering data about our entertainment choices, some satellite companies are able to suggest programmes we may like to watch based on our previous viewing patterns. It is also possible for TV programmes to be made based purely on data that has been collected and analysed. For example, the original show *The House of Cards* was commissioned by Netflix purely on the analysed data relating to the viewing habits of its subscribers.

Music streaming websites such as Spotify can suggest tracks and artists we may like to listen to based on our past music download choices.

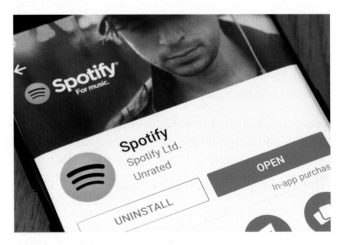

Figure 3.7 A streaming service

By analysing the collected data, media companies can predict what type of programmes, films and music people want to watch or listen to. By looking at viewing histories, searches, reviews and ratings, and even the device the content is watched or listened to on, producers can aim to provide media that is wanted.

The data can also be used to analyse at what time people are most likely to watch films or programmes and what device they will be using when they view it. It is also possible to use the analysed data to provide advertising that is based on, for example, the age group of the people who are watching.

Activity

In groups, select two different entertainment areas and investigate how data can be used to influence the content. Report your findings back to the class.

Lifestyle

The use of data related to lifestyle is huge. Applications vary, from cars that can automatically call for help to solar panels on house roofs feeding power back into the National Grid. Social media also collects, processes and analyses data and information from users.

Some cars have an SOS button, which when pressed sends a signal to the manufacturer assistance team. When the signal is received, the position of the car is also provided so that help and assistance can be sent. The registration number of the car will be located and, if up-to-date contact details are available, the owner of the car can be contacted.

Many cars have a tracking system built in. The tracking system, if activated if the car is stolen, can send a signal to the tracking system assistance team and the police. The signal sent by the tracking system can show the location of the car and, if it is being driven, the route being taken. This sharing of data can help recover stolen cars.

Figure 3.8 An SOS button

Green energy is the use of natural, renewable resources to generate power. Some houses have solar panels on the roof. When the sun shines on the panels, electricity is generated. This electricity is used by the house but sometimes too much is generated. If this happens then the electricity is fed back into the National Grid to add to the electricity supply. Data is collected from the houses that feed electricity into the National Grid. This data can be analysed to see where the best places for solar panels to be located are, how much energy is generated by the solar panels and what percentage of the electricity needs of the UK is met by the generation of electricity by solar panels.

Figure 3.9 Solar panels on a house roof

Connected houses also supply and use data. Many houses now have smart meters, which send readings every few seconds of how much gas and electricity is being used. This data is used by the suppliers to provide accurate bills to the customer. The data can also be analysed by the suppliers, for example, to see at what time of day and night the most or least gas and electricity is being used.

This analysed data can help suppliers forecast how much gas and electricity they will need to supply in future months. The data can also be used to see the changes in usage as the weather turns colder or hotter.

Some connected houses also have connected door locks. These locks can report to the owner of the house and the security company if there is any movement into or out of the house, for example when the owners are on holiday. This data can be fed back to the security company who will then alert the police to go and check that the house hasn't been burgled. This data could be used by insurance companies to find out which areas are the least and most likely to be burgled. The insurance companies could then use this data to set prices for home insurance.

 Activity

Investigate the devices that can be installed in a connected house. Find out the purpose of each device and think about what data could be sent back to the manufacturer or supplier.

Another way that lifestyle data can be collected is through the use of social media. Social media is seen as one of the most significant sources of Big Data. Data is collected every time someone likes or dislikes a page, video or photograph. Data is also collected each time a page, photograph or video is shared, followed, retweeted or commented on.

The data collected by the actions of social media users can help marketing companies to target products. For example, data collected could be analysed to find out which age group and gender could best be targeted with a discount on gym membership.

 Activity

Look at a range of social media apps. Think about how the actions of a user could result in targeted advertisements and offers.

Benefits and drawbacks of the use of data

You have learned that data can be collected, stored, processed and analysed. But, to get the best results, the data must be correct.

Some of the *benefits* of using data include:

- large amounts of data can be found using a range of data stores
- searches can be made to find the specific data required
- time does not have to be wasted collecting new data
- data can be shared by teams carrying out the same tasks
- a range of different analyses can be carried out on data
- data stores can interact to share data.

It is important to remember that in most of the areas looked at earlier in this section, the data stores will interact with at least one other, for example the police and the DVLA.

 Activity

Think about other data stores that could interact. How do they interact, what data do they share and why?

Some of the *drawbacks* to the use of data include:

- it is not always possible to know if the data is correct, if it has been gathered by someone else
- errors in the data can have a negative impact on people

- it may not be possible to get the specific data required
- data must be kept up to date, with the data owners being informed when updates are made
- incorrect data can lead to incorrect results (**GIGO**)
- sensitive data must be securely stored with good data security measures.

Key term

GIGO Garbage In, Garbage Out.

Activity

Think about the use of data by the police. Consider what would happen if the data held by the DVLA about a personalised car registration plate had been updated but the owner of the data had not been informed.

Practice questions

1 Identify and describe **two** ways in which Big Data could be used in the area of shopping. [6 marks]

2 Explain how the data produced by a smart meter can be used by the gas and electricity supplier. [4 marks]

3 Describe **two** drawbacks of using secondary research methods to collect data. [4 marks]

LO4

Understand the factors to be considered when collecting and processing data and storing data/information

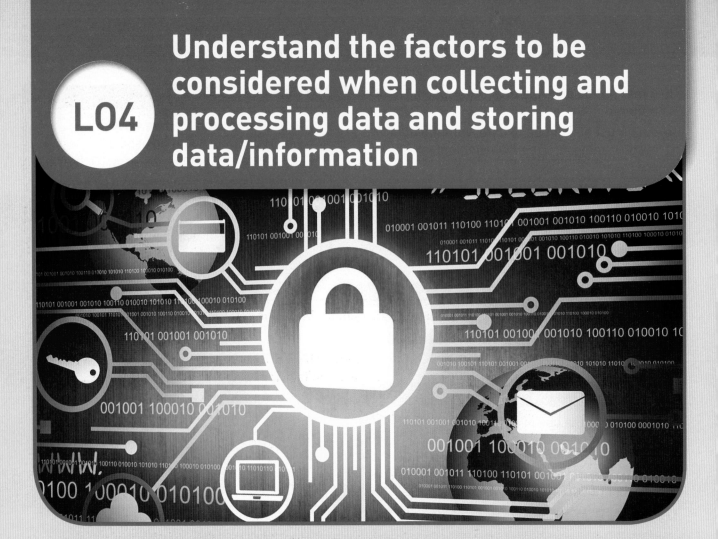

About this chapter

There are many different types of threat to data that is stored, on both the cloud and on physical storage devices. You will learn about some of the different threats and the vulnerabilities that can lead to these threats being carried out.

These threats must be considered when data is being collected, stored and processed. Data and information may include people's personal data, so it is important that it is kept as safe as possible. Threats can be reduced by using protection measures.

You will learn about the different protection measures that can be put in place. If someone steals data through a cyber-security attack, then that could have a severe impact on people or businesses.

There are several pieces of legislation that relate to cyber-security attacks and keeping data and information safe. You will learn about this legislation and how it can be used to deal with cyber-security attackers. You will also learn about the legislation that should be considered when data and information is being collected and processed.

If secondary research is being carried out using external sources, factors related to these sources and the data and information they contain should also be considered.

Chapter content

4.1 Types of threats

4.2 The vulnerabilities that can be exploited in a cyber-security attack

4.3 The impacts and consequences of a cyber-security attack

4.4 Prevention measures

4.5 Current relevant IT legislation, its implications and applications

4.6 The importance of validity, reliability and bias when collecting and using data and information

4.1 Types of threats

There are many different threats to data and information. Some threats can also be targeted at physical computer equipment.

Cyber-security attackers can hijack a computer system, which can lead to data and information being stolen. The impact of this can be huge for a business or an individual. As more businesses and people use the internet for financial transactions, security of this data has to be increased to ensure that information and data does not fall into the wrong hands.

Some of the most common threats to data security and computer systems are botnets and the different types of malware.

Malware

Malware (malicious software) is installed on a computer system and collects information about users without their knowledge. There are many types of malware but the main types are adware, bot, bug, ransomware, rootkit, spyware, Trojan horse, virus and worm (see Table 4.1). A botnet is an interconnected network of several computers infected by bot malware. This allows the botnet, and the person who created it, to take control of the computer systems.

It is simple to protect against many forms of malware by installing, running and keeping updated security software. It is also not wise to open any suspicious files or click on any links in emails.

Table 4.1 The types of malware

Type of malware	Why it is used	How it works	How to mitigate
Adware	Adware generates revenue for its author	Adware is also known as advertising-supported software. This is any software package that automatically shows adverts, such as pop-ups. It may also be in the user interface of a software package or on an installation screen. Adware, by itself, is harmless; however, some adware may include spyware such as key loggers.	Install, run and keep updated a security software package Do not open any files from an unknown source Do not click any links in emails
Bot	Bots take control of a computer system	A bot is a type of malware that allows a cyber-security attacker to take control of an infected computer system without the user's knowledge. It can result in a botnet which is an interconnected network of infected computer systems.	Install, run and keep updated a security software package Do not open any files from an unknown source Do not click any links in emails

Continued

Table 4.1 Continued

Type of malware	Why it is used	How it works	How to mitigate
Bug	Bugs are connected to software and are a flaw that produces an unwanted outcome	Bugs are usually the result of human error during the coding of the software. Most bugs can be fixed by the software creator issuing a fix or patch. Security bugs are the most severe type and can allow cyber attackers to bypass user authentication, override access privileges or steal data.	Check for and install any patches that are released from software vendors
Ransomware	Ransomware holds a computer system captive and demands a ransom, usually money, to release it	Ransomware can restrict user access to the computer system by encrypting files or locking down the computer system. A message is usually displayed to force the user to pay so that the restrictions can be lifted and the user has access to the data or computer system. It is spread like a worm and can be started by downloading an infected file or by a vulnerability on the computer system.	Do not open any files from an unknown source Do not click any links in emails Install, run and keep updated a security software package
Rootkit	A rootkit is designed to remotely access or control a computer system without being detected by the security software or the user	When a rootkit has been installed it can enable a cyber attacker to remotely access files, access/ steal data and information, modify software configurations or control the computer system as part of a botnet.	Rootkits are difficult to detect as they are not usually detected by security software Software updates, keeping security software up to date and not downloading suspicious files are the only ways of trying to avoid a rootkit from being installed
Spyware	Spyware can collect data from an infected computer, including personal information like websites visited, user logins and financial information	Spyware is usually hidden from a user and can be difficult to detect. It is often secretly installed on a user's personal computer without their knowledge. Some spyware such as key loggers, however, may be installed intentionally to monitor users. Spyware can also install additional software or redirect web browsers to different websites. Some spyware can change computer settings, which could lead to slow internet connection speeds or changes in web browser settings.	Do not open any files from an unknown source Do not click any links in emails Install, run and keep updated a security software package
Trojan horse	A Trojan horse is a standalone malicious program designed to give full control of an infected PC to another PC	Trojans often appear to be something that is wanted or needed by the user of a PC. They can be hidden in valid programs and software. Trojan horses can make copies of themselves, steal information, or harm the host computer systems.	Do not open any files from an unknown source Do not click any links in emails Install, run and keep updated a security software package

Continued

Table 4.1 Continued

Type of malware	Why it is used	How it works	How to mitigate
Virus	A virus attempts to make a computer system unreliable	A virus is a computer program that replicates itself and spreads from computer to computer. Viruses can increase their chances of spreading to other computers by infecting files on a network file system or a file system that is accessed by other computers.	Do not open any files from an unknown source Do not click any links in emails Install, run and keep updated a security software package
Worm	A worm is a standalone computer program that replicates itself so it can spread to other computers	A worm can use a computer network to spread. Unlike a computer virus, it does not need to attach itself to an existing program. Worms almost always cause some harm to a network, even if only by consuming bandwidth.	Do not open any files from an unknown source Do not click any links in emails Install, run and keep updated a security software package

Social engineering

Social engineering is the art of manipulating people so that confidential information can be found out. It can take many forms. The most common ones are described in Table 4.2.

Table 4.2 Types of social engineering

Type of social engineering	Why it is used	How it works
Phishing	Phishing tries to get users to input their credit or debit card numbers, or security details or log-in details into a fake website	Phishing uses a fake website that looks identical to the real one. The most common targets for phishing are bank, building society and insurance websites. For example, the attackers send out emails or SMS that pretend to be from a bank. A link is contained in the email, which the user is asked to click on. This link takes the user to a fake website.
Pretexting	Pretexting is when a cybercriminal lies to get data or information	Pretexting usually involves a scam where the criminal pretends to need the information to confirm the identity of the person they are talking to.
Baiting	Baiting tries to get victims to give cybercriminals the information they need	Baiting is very similar to phishing. The cybercriminals make a promise of goods to get the information they need. An example would be to promise free downloads of films or music in return for log-in details.
Quid pro quo	Quid pro quo tries to disable anti-virus software so that software updates, usually malware, can be installed to gain access to a computer system	Quid pro quo is very similar to baiting, except the promise is that of a service rather than goods. A common method is a telephone call claiming to be from an IT service provider. These people offer assistance in fixing IT problems.
Tailgating/piggybacking	Tailgating/piggybacking means trying to gain access to a secure building or room	Tailgating/piggybacking takes the form of someone who does not have authority to enter a building or room, following someone who does through the doors. The most common type is an attacker pretending to be a delivery driver and asking an authorised person to hold the door.
Shoulder surfing	Shoulder surfing aims to steal data and information	Shoulder surfing is when a person's private and confidential information is seen. For example, an attacker may stand very close to someone using a cash machine in order to see their PIN. This is very effective in crowded places when a person uses a smartphone or mobile device and log-in details can be seen.

Figure 4.1 Social engineering

Activity

Identify a method that could be used to mitigate against each type of social engineering shown in Table 4.2.

Activity

It is sometimes very difficult to tell real from fake websites that are used for phishing. In pairs, make a list of the things you could check to see if a website is legitimate.

Hacking

Hacking means finding weaknesses in an established system and exploiting them, for example, to gain unauthorised access. A hacker may be motivated by a multitude of reasons, such as profit, protest or challenge.

There are three main types of hacking that can take place.

White hat hacking

This is where the hacker is given permission to hack into systems to identify any loopholes or vulnerabilities. As this type of hacking is done with the permission of the computer system owner, it does not break any of the legislation that relates to hacking. White hat hackers are motivated to keep the system as safe as possible from malicious hacking attempts.

Grey hat hacking

This is where the hacker hacks into computer systems for fun or to troll but without malicious intent towards the computer system. If a grey hat hacker finds a weakness then they may offer to fix the vulnerability – for a fee! Grey hat hackers can also manipulate the rankings of websites when a search is done on a search engine.

Black hat hacking

This is where the hacker hacks into a computer system with malicious intent. This intent can include theft, exploiting the data stolen or seen, and selling the data on. Black hat hackers carry out illegal hacking activities and can be prosecuted under UK IT legislation.

Links to other sections

You will learn more about UK IT legislation in Section 4.5 of this chapter.

Distributed denial of service (DDoS)

Distributed denial of service (DDoS) is an attempt to make a computer or network system unavailable to its users by flooding it with network traffic. A DDoS is usually focused on preventing an internet site or service from functioning efficiently, or at all, either temporarily or indefinitely. The attacks usually target sites or services hosted on high-profile web servers such as banks, payment websites (e.g. PayPal) and mobile phone companies.

Pharming

Pharming is a cyber-security attack that tries to redirect visitors from a genuine website to a fake one. This is done without the knowledge or consent of the users. There are some similarities between phishing and pharming. Fraudulent websites are used by attackers carrying out both phishing and pharming attacks, but phishing attacks use fake or hoax emails.

Practice questions

1 Describe the difference between white hat hacking and black hat hacking.   [4 marks]
2 Identify and describe **one** type of malware.   [3 marks]
3 Describe what is meant by the social engineering technique of pretexting. Identify **one** method that could be used to mitigate the risk of pretexting.   [4 marks]

4.2 The vulnerabilities that can be exploited in a cyber-security attack

A vulnerability is a weakness that allows an attacker to launch a cyber-security attack. There are three categories of vulnerability that you need to be aware of:

● environmental
● physical
● system.

Some organisations run vulnerability testing when a computer system is being created and installed. It is also possible to run vulnerability testing once a computer system is running. These tests can identify vulnerabilities and steps can be taken to rectify these before a cyber-security attack is successful.

The vulnerability that can affect computer devices and systems the most, however, is the behaviour of users of the computer system. Users must be aware of the vulnerabilities so that they do not cause any issue that compromises the computer devices, the system, or the data and information.

Environmental

With the increase in the use of mobile computer devices and the cloud, there are environmental vulnerabilities that can affect data, information and computer systems.

If a natural disaster occurred, for example, an earthquake, it is probable that internet access would be lost. This would make any data and information stored in the cloud inaccessible. The impact of inaccessible data and information could affect recovery from a natural disaster, for example if it was data stored by a government about the location and number of people in remote villages. If this information was lost in a natural disaster, any rescuers might not know how many people they were looking for.

It is also possible that computer devices could be destroyed during a natural disaster. If a tsunami or flood occurred, the water coming on to the land could destroy or wash away buildings. Computer devices in these buildings would be destroyed or lost. The cabling infrastructure or any internet service equipment could also be affected. It may be, however, that buildings remain safe but the tremors that happen with a natural disaster like an earthquake do damage to hard drive surfaces, making the data and information stored on them unreadable.

Even if physical backups were available on physical storage media such as flash drives or external hard drives, there is a chance that these would also be affected by the same natural disaster. If the backups were stored in the cloud, these would be inaccessible if there was no internet access.

One of the after-effects of a natural disaster may be power failure, as happened when hurricane Irma struck the Caribbean islands in 2017. As computer systems need electricity, either to charge or operate, power failures mean very limited accessibility to data and information and the computer devices these are stored on. One way to keep computer systems operating is to use batteries or a power generator as back-up power sources. The batteries must be kept fully charged, however, with fuel available to run the generator.

Another natural disaster that could affect computer systems and devices is lightning strikes. A lightning strike can cause a surge or spike in the electricity supply. These surges can affect how hard drives and other storage devices operate.

Activity

Investigate the different devices that can be used to protect against power surges. Identify where each device could be used, for example in a large or small business or in a house.

Physical

Some vulnerabilities relate to the physical devices that can be used to store and process data and information. Physical vulnerabilities can also lead to the theft of identity.

Links to other sections

You will learn more about identity theft in Section 4.3 of this chapter.

The most common vulnerability relating to computer devices and portable storage media is theft. Theft can occur because of someone breaking into a business's office and stealing devices. An authorised user may lose a computer or portable storage device, for example, by leaving it on a train or at an airport. If this happens and someone else picks up the computer or device, the contents may be used for illegal activity. However, there is always a chance that the item will be handed in to the police so that it can be returned to its owner.

There have been some high-profile cases where computer devices and portable storage have been left in public places, for example, in 2008 a memory stick was found in a pub car park. The memory stick contained passwords for HM Government Gateway, an online system run by the government that allows people to claim for state benefits and file tax returns.

Activity

Using the BBC News website and other websites, investigate cases where computer and storage devices have been found by members of the public.

System

Some vulnerabilities relate to the running of the devices and the computer system. One vulnerability relates to the use of weak passwords.

Links to other sections

You will learn more about passwords in Section 4.4 of this chapter.

User IDs and passwords are provided by businesses to their computer users, but passwords can be changed to something that the user can remember. A weak password is one that is easy to find out or guess, by people and by computers. Passwords are often changed to obvious words and numbers, such as the name of a user's children and house number. The simpler the password, the easier it is to guess. This is a vulnerability caused by users.

It is important that software is updated. Most software vendors issue updates for their software following its release. These updates are called 'patches'. Many patches attempt to resolve potential vulnerabilities that may have been identified by either the vendors or by users of the software. The updating of software – operating systems and security software – can be done automatically or manually.

Many operating systems have the facility to update automatically. This usually happens as the computer system is going through the shutdown process. When the computer system has reached a point specified by the software vendor, the operating system downloads any updates that have become available since the last shutdown process was carried out.

Figure 4.2 The Windows update screen

At the end of the updating procedure the computer system will automatically shut down without any intervention from the user. By using the automatic updating facility, the user does not have to remember to update – the computer system will automatically carry out the procedure.

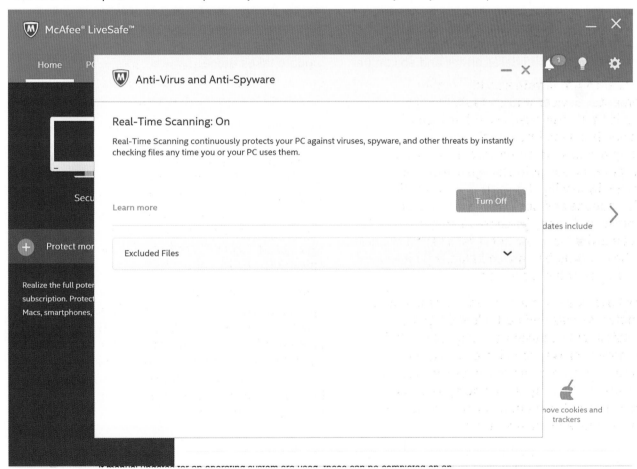

Figure 4.3 Real-time scanning of security software

Some security software will also update automatically. This process is usually completed in real time. This means that when the computer system is connected to the internet, the security software will constantly be checking for new updates. If an update is found then the security software will automatically install it. This happens because new viruses, and other security threats covered by the software, are being released all the time.

Like with the automatic updates for the operating system, this means that the user does not have to remember to manually check for updates and so the computer system is always protected from any threats.

In the same way, if a business uses automatic updates of operating systems and security software, it does not have to remember to manually check for updates either and so can be sure that its computer system is as up to date as possible. This also means that any vulnerabilities identified by the vendor are solved before a cyber-security attack can take place.

Manually updating operating systems and security software can be dangerous to the computer system and the data that is held on it. This is because a manual update can be forgotten by an employee and this can leave the computer system vulnerable to threats.

If manual updates for an operating system are used, these can be completed on an ad-hoc basis or can be set to check at a time specified by a user. One of the problems with manually updating software is the time it can take to download the patch. Another problem is that there may be a time delay between the patch being released by the software vendor and the time the manual update takes place.

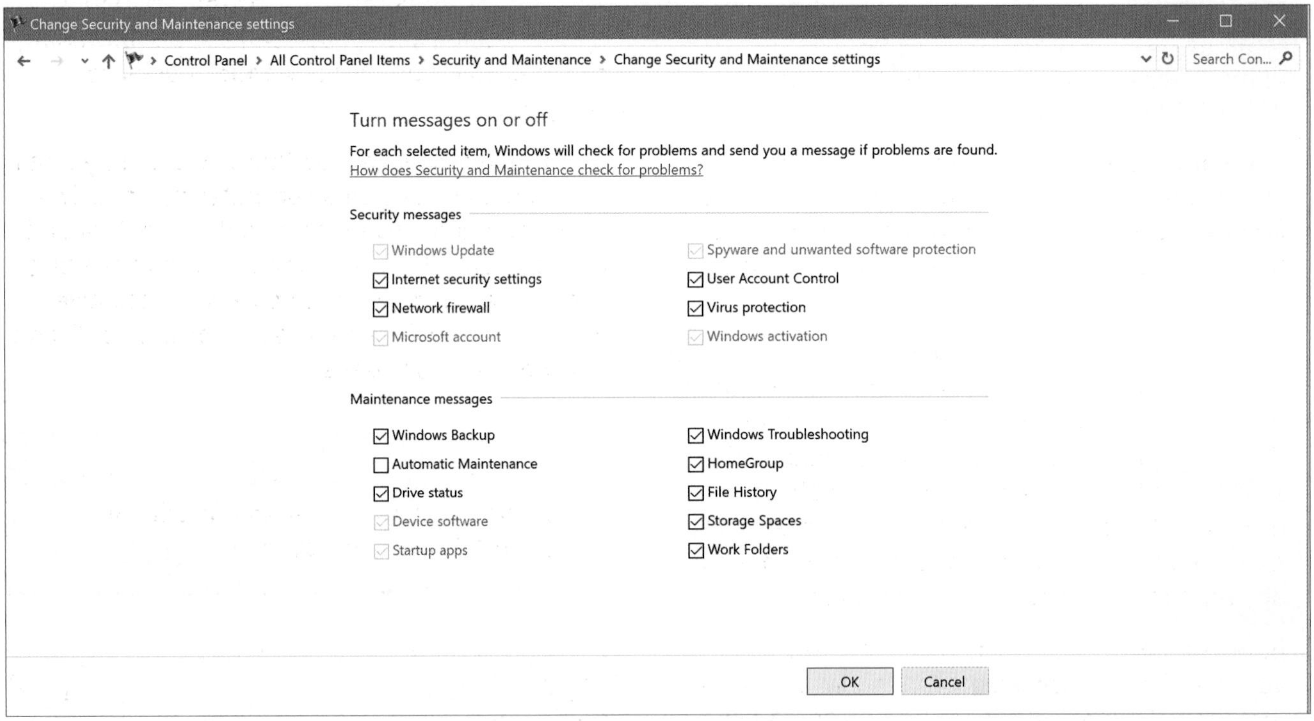

Figure 4.4 Settings for manual updating of software

Automatic Maintenance

Windows automatically runs scheduled maintenance on a daily schedule when you're not using your computer.

This includes tasks such as software updates, security scanning, and system diagnostics. This maintenance will run daily if you aren't using your computer at the time you've chosen. If your computer is in use at the scheduled time or maintenance is behind schedule, Automatic Maintenance will run the next time the computer is not being used.

Automatic Maintenance

Run maintenance tasks daily at 02:00 ⌄

☐ Allow scheduled maintenance to wake up my computer at the scheduled time

---

Figure 4.5 Settings for scheduled updates

Another problem with manually scheduling updates is that the computer system must be switched on and connected to the internet for the update to be downloaded. If the manual update has been scheduled for a time of day when the business computer system is switched off, the business will never get updates or patches downloaded. This can leave the computer system open to attacks and threats and could result in data being lost or stolen.

Some users, however, may decide to manually update software because they want to look at the updates to decide whether or not to download them. Some users may consider updates to be intrusive or not appropriate.

Security software can also be manually updated or scheduled to download updates. As with manually updating the operating system, this can leave the computer system vulnerable to attacks. For example, if the updates are checked at 5 p.m. each evening and new viruses are released overnight, then the computer system will have no protection against these all through the working day.

Insecure hardware can also cause system vulnerabilities. Wireless internet connections are increasingly popular in both homes and offices. It is very common for some businesses, for example, coffee shops or hotels, to offer Wi-Fi access to their customers. Some of these Wi-Fi

connections are unsecured, meaning a user ID or password is not needed to join the connection. Unsecured modems, hubs and routers can mean that the internet access or the computer devices connected to Wi-Fi are vulnerable to a cyber-security attack. A device connected to Wi-Fi can be accessed, with the data and information it contains being able to be seen. This vulnerability can make a cyber-security attack easier to carry out.

You have already learned that vulnerability testing can identify issues on a computer system. The weakest link of any system containing data and information is the user, and social engineering tries to persuade users to part with sensitive information such as their password, user ID and any other access codes.

Links to other sections

You learned about social engineering in Section 4.1 of this chapter.

Activity

Think about some scenarios when social engineering could be used to gain sensitive information.

4.3 The impacts and consequences of a cyber-security attack

The impacts of a cyber-security attack

If a cyber-security attack takes place and is successful, this can have an impact on businesses and individuals. Sometimes a successful attack on a business can have an impact on both the business and its customers.

Denial of service attack

A denial of service attack can have an impact on the authorised users of the website that is being attacked. This can lead to authorised users being unable to access the website while it is under attack or after the attack has finished. For example, if a banking website was the victim of a DoS attack then customers who use that bank website would be unable to access their accounts, pay bills, transfer money or complete other online banking activities. In December 2015 the BBC was the victim of a DoS attack, with iPlayer being taken offline, preventing online viewing of BBC news and other programming.

Identify theft

Identify theft is one result of a cyber-security attack. Identity theft is when personal details are stolen, and identity fraud is when those details are used to commit fraud, for example taking out

a loan in someone else's name. If cyber-security attackers get hold of a someone's name, address and date of birth then this is enough for them to create a copy of that person. If a person's identity is stolen then this could result in, for example, big debts being run up in their name or passports being issued and possibly used for criminal activity. A very high profile case happened in 2001, when a man called Abraham Abdallah stole the identities of several famous and wealthy people, including Stephen Spielberg, to attempt to steal millions of dollars.

Whenever data is being stored, it is at risk of a cyber-security attack. During an attack, data could be destroyed, manipulated, modified or stolen.

Links to other sections

You will learn more about the legislation that must be considered when storing personal details in Section 4.5 of this chapter.

Data destruction

Data destruction is when data is destroyed by a cyber-security attacker and no longer exists.

Data manipulation

Data manipulation is when data is edited, usually to meet the needs of cyber-security attackers. For example, the attackers could change the data in a news feed on Twitter or Facebook. This could result in false news being published on these social media platforms. This is type of cyber-security attack is usually found quite quickly.

Data modification

Data modification also changes data to meet the needs of the attacker, for example, changing the amount of money in a bank account. The attacker can then withdraw the increased amount of money, causing the bank to lose money. In some cases, the crime may not be found for a long time. Data modification is very similar to data manipulation but the attackers usually have different aims.

Data theft

Data theft is when cyber-security attackers steal computer-based data from a person or business, with the intent of compromising privacy or obtaining confidential data. Data that can be stolen includes passwords, personal details and financial data. Data theft can also be committed by stealing portable storage devices or mobile devices such as laptops and tablets.

Links to other sections

You will learn more about the different protection measures that can be used against cyber-security attacks in Section 4.4 of this chapter.

The consequences of a cyber-security attack

Any cyber-security attack can have consequences, which can be related to loss, disruption or safety. Each of these can in turn can have consequences on different areas.

Loss

Many cyber-security attacks result in data and information being stolen or corrupted so it can no longer be used. If there is a backup then it is possible to restore the data and information, but most businesses back up only once a day. This means that at least one day's data and information will have been lost or corrupted.

Links to other sections

You will learn more about backups in Section 4.4 of this chapter.

There are three main consequences resulting from the loss of data: financial, data and reputation.

Financial

When data and information is lost or corrupted, a business can suffer financially. For example, accounts records may be lost and it is also possible that invoices created on the day of the attack may be lost or corrupted. This would mean that records of who owes the business money would need to be recreated. There is always a possibility that, depending on the data that was lost or corrupted, not all invoices can be recreated, so resulting in a loss of income for the business.

If personal data is targeted during the attack, then the business may also have to pay compensation to the people whose data has been lost. Legislation requires businesses to pay compensation to the people whose data has been lost, stolen or corrupted. This compensation can be very high, sometimes running into thousands of pounds. If more than one person's data has been lost or stolen then this sum of money will increase. The cost of this compensation may result in the business having to be shut down if it does not have enough money to pay the compensation or to carry on trading.

Links to other sections

You will learn more about IT legislation in Section 4.5 of this chapter.

Another increased cost may be that the business will have to raise the level of security of its computer systems. This can be expensive as new software and hardware may have to be bought. There is also the additional cost of the installation and maintenance of this hardware and software.

There is a high risk that the customers of the business will lose confidence in it and take their custom elsewhere. This can, again, lead to financial worry for the business and, without customers, it may not be able to carry on trading.

People may also suffer financial problems if their data is lost. If this included sensitive data, such as name, address and date of birth, then criminals could use that information to, for example, get credit cards or loans. The person whose data was used might have no idea until credit card statements or other letters arrive at their address. It is then very difficult to prove that the card or loan was taken out by someone else.

Data

You have already learned how the loss of data can have financial consequences. While many businesses do back up their data, the timing of the backups can lead to data loss. The data that has been lost may not just be accounts data; it is possible that supplier and customer data may also be lost. This, as you have already learned, may have financial consequences for the business.

There is always a time delay before the most recent backup can be used to reinstate data. This delay can have consequences for how the business is able to interact with its customers and suppliers. With many business transactions happening online, for example, e-commerce, customer orders may be lost. The loss of this data can have consequences for customers as their personal data and the goods they ordered may be lost.

Emails and contact lists can also be targeted during a cyber-security attack. The loss of email addresses and contact information could result in a business not being able to fully function, so losing money and possibly going out of business.

If customers' data is lost then this may have a devastating consequence. The loss of personal data could result in identity theft. The other consequence of data loss is financial, as you learned in the section about the financial impact above.

Links to other sections

You learned about identity theft earlier in Section 4.3.

Reputation

If a business has been the target of a cyber-security attack and data has been lost, then its reputation will be negatively affected. It is very likely that the business will no longer be seen as trustworthy by its customers and the confidence that they had in the business will reduce. This could mean customers moving their custom to a different business, which could lead to the business stopping trading.

For example, supermarkets hold details of customers who use their delivery service. If this data was lost, stolen or corrupted, then customers may find another supermarket to do their deliveries.

Top tip

You may need to know about the consequences of data loss for both individuals and businesses for your exam, R012.

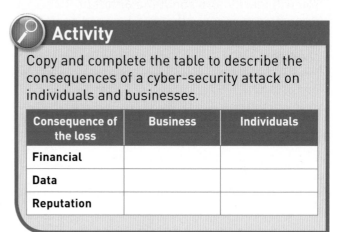

Activity

Copy and complete the table to describe the consequences of a cyber-security attack on individuals and businesses.

Consequence of the loss	Business	Individuals
Financial		
Data		
Reputation		

Disruption

A cyber-security attack will always cause some level of disruption, both when the attack is taking place and after it has happened. There are three main consequences resulting from the disruption caused by a cyber-security attack: operational, financial and commercial.

Operational

You have already learned that a cyber-security attack can result in lost or corrupt data. The business may have backups, but the time taken to reinstall the data can have an impact on its operations. A business relies on data to carry out its day-to-day functions, both internally and in the interaction between it and its suppliers and/or customers.

The time delay in restoring lost or corrupted data will mean that the business cannot carry out its day-to-day business. While the business is recovering from the cyber-attack it may not be able to operate, as the internal data required to be shared between departments and external data, such as links with suppliers and customers, may be lost or corrupt. This will have a negative consequence for the business and can cause disruption to its function.

Financial

You have already learned about the possible financial consequences to a business of a cyber-security attack. A cyber-security attack can impact negatively on a business's finances, as you learned earlier in this section. To recap, the financial consequences of a cyber-security attack include:

- loss of customers, leading to loss of revenue
- possible payment of compensation
- increased costs to improve security and computer devices, including installation and maintenance
- loss of revenue, for example, if invoices are lost.

Commercial

The biggest consequence for a business of a cyber-security attack is on its day-to-day running. When a cyber-security attack is happening, or after it has happened, the business may be unable to function.

Activity

In groups, discuss what would happen if the air traffic control system for Heathrow Airport was the victim of a cyber-security attack.

The commercial consequence of the cyber-security attack would depend on the function of the business.

It would be devastating if the nuclear power station at Sellafield were to be the victim of an attack. This would not only affect the day-to-day running of the power station but could also have serious consequences for the safety of the north-west of England.

It would be less catastrophic, but no less serious, if a supermarket chain were the victim of an attack. Although it is possible that customer details could be stolen, a supermarket would still be able to function with limited commercial consequences.

Activity

Copy and complete the table to describe the consequences of disruption following a cyber-security attack.

Consequence of the disruption	Business	Individuals
Operational		
Financial		
Commercial		

Top tip

You may need to know about the consequences of disruption for both individuals and businesses for your exam, R012.

Safety

A cyber-security attack can have serious effects on various aspects of safety. However, the systems that are linked with safety are very well protected against cyber-security attacks, with logical and physical protection measures.

Links to other sections

You will learn more about the prevention measures that could be used against a cyber-security attack in Section 4.4 of this chapter.

The safety of individuals, equipment and finance is at risk if targeted by a cyber-security attack.

Individuals

You have already learned about the devastating effects that could occur because of a cyber-security attack.

With the increased use of the internet and Big Data stores, most businesses, government departments and the armed forces are connected in some way. A targeted cyber-security attack on a government website and the data held by that department could have an impact on national security.

Activity

During May 2017, the NHS was the victim of a cyber-security attack. In groups, investigate the effects this attack could have had on patient safety and the impact on the day-to-day running of a hospital. Present your findings to the rest of the class.

For example, if the cyber-security attack was targeted at the prison service this could result in prisoners being released early. This could put the safety of the general population at risk.

A targeted attack on the railway system could also have catastrophic results. Signals on the train tracks may not work properly, which could result in two trains travelling in opposite directions being on the same part of a train track at the same time.

Activity

Make a list of other organisations that could be targeted to have an impact on people's safety.

The loss or corruption of personal data could result in personal details becoming known to the attackers. This could lead to identity theft.

For example, in April 2017 the loan firm Wonga was the victim of a cyber-security attack. The data of more than 250,000 people who had used the firm was stolen. All these people risked having their identities misused as a result of this attack.

Such data could be sold to criminals on the dark web, which could result in their houses and cars being burgled.

Equipment

During a cyber-security attack, equipment such as computer devices, including internet-access devices, could be targeted. This could take the form of a Distributed Denial of Service (DDoS) attack.

Links to other sections

You learned about DDoS attacks in Section 4.1 of this chapter.

If computer devices are targeted, a business or individual may not be able to carry out any tasks because the equipment may not be functioning correctly. For example, if an individual's hub has been targeted then they may not be able to access the internet to carry out tasks such as online banking or shopping using e-commerce websites.

If an internet device connected to a business has been targeted then the business may not be able to access any data and information stored in the cloud, or to receive orders from customers or access supplier websites.

There are other types of equipment that could be targeted. For example, you learned earlier in this section that equipment related to safety can be impacted during in cyber-security attack.

Finance

The impact of a cyber-security attack on finance can occur both while the attack is taking place and after.

While a cyber-security attack is happening, access may be denied to websites such as banking. If a business loses personal data during the attack then this can have an impact on its finances. You learned about this earlier in this section.

If this loss of personal data resulted in identity theft occurring, then there would also be a financial impact on the person whose identity has been stolen. You learned about identity theft earlier in this section.

Activity

Copy and complete the table to describe the consequences for safety following a cyber-security attack.

Consequence for safety	Business	Individuals
Individuals		
Equipment		
Finance		

Top tip

You may need to know about the consequences of cyber-security attacks for safety for both individuals and businesses for your exam, R012.

Practice questions

1 An online shopping website has suffered a cyber-security attack and customer data has been stolen.

    Describe **two** impacts for the customers of having their data stolen. **[4 marks]**

2 Explain the impact on a banking website of a DDoS attack. **[4 marks]**

3 Discuss the consequences of a cyber-security attack on the reputation of a large business. **[8 marks]**

4.4 Prevention measures

When data and information is stored it needs to be protected to keep it safe.

Links to other sections

You learned about some of the threats to data and information in Section 4.1 of this chapter.

There are different ways in which data and information can be protected.

Physical

There are many physical protection measures that can be taken. The choice of measure will depend on the device being protected.

Biometric protection measures

Some devices include biometric protection measures. A biometric protection measure uses a physical characteristic of the user, for example, a fingerprint, eye scan or voice.

It is common for laptops, smartphones and tablets to need a biometric measure to be positive before the device can be accessed. The owner of the device will have stored their characteristic as part of the security settings on the device. For example, when a fingerprint is used to access the device, this is checked against the stored fingerprint and if there is a match, then access is granted. This means that only people whose characteristic is stored and recognised can access the device. If anyone else tries to gain access, the characteristic will not be recognised and access will be denied.

Large businesses can use biometric protection measures, for example, to protect server rooms. When someone tries to access this room, they must scan their fingerprint, for example. This is then checked against the database of authorised personnel fingerprints and, if there is a match, access will be granted.

There are some disadvantages to using biometric protection measures, for example, a person's voice can change if they have a cold. This can cause problems if the device they are trying to access does not recognise the voice pattern. People can injure their fingers, for example, with a burn or cut. This can change the pattern of the fingerprint and may result in access being denied. Another example may be if someone has been swimming and their fingers get wet and wrinkly. This will change the pattern of the fingerprint and result in the scanner not recognising the fingerprint.

There are several other physical protection measures that can be used.

- Locking doors when rooms containing computer equipment are not in use.
- Using swipe or **RFID** cards or keypads to activate locks.
- Bolting computer equipment to desks.
- Using special pens to mark the postcode on computer equipment.
- Using CCTV cameras.
- Closing windows and blinds when rooms are not in use.

Key term

RFID Radio Frequency Identification Tags can use radio frequency to transfer data from the tags to a computer system, for example to allow access to a room.

Top tip

You will need to keep up to date with emerging technologies that can be used as physical protection measures.

Logical

There are many logical protection measures that can be taken. The choice of measure will depend on the data and information being protected.

Access rights and permissions

Computer systems and files and folders containing data and information have **access rights** and **permissions**, which can be adjusted to control who can read, edit or alter and save the file. Authentication and usernames and passwords can be used to set access rights and permissions for each person.

Key terms

Access rights Control over who has access to a computer system, folder, files, data and/or information.

Permissions A set of attributes that determine what a user can do with files and folders, for example, read, write, edit or delete.

Authentication

Some access systems use two-step authentication as another layer of logical protection. The most common authentication protection is that of using a token. When a user tries to access a secure area, the username and password is entered. When these are submitted and checked, the system creates a token code, usually made up of numbers, which is sent to the email address (or by text message to the mobile phone number) linked to the username and password. To access the secure area, the user must input the token code.

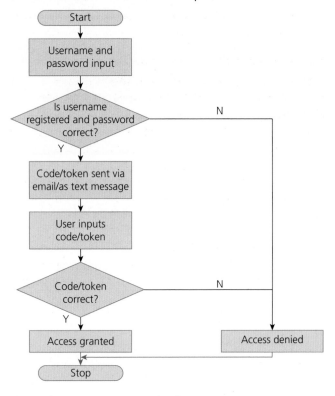

Figure 4.6 Two-step authentication

Usernames and passwords

Usernames and passwords are a two-part logical protection measure. The username acts as authorisation while the password acts as authentication. Without both parts being correct, access will be denied to a computer system that is used to store data and information.

The username is a unique identifier for a user and identifies who the user is to the computer system. The username can be allocated to a group, for example, in your school a group of teachers and a group of students. Each group will have access rights and software allocated to them.

The password is the method of restricting access. Without the correct password being linked to the correct username, access is denied. The password lets the system know that the user is who the username says they are.

Activity

It is essential that any password used is strong. In pairs, create a list of rules that should be followed when choosing a strong password. Discuss your findings with another group.

A business can use access rights and permissions to control which files employees are allowed to look at by setting different access permissions to the folders or files. Managers can have access to folders of files that other office staff do not – a personnel manager would be able to look into the files and folders that contain staff personal details, but a warehouse manager would not have the access rights and permissions to do this.

Files and folders can be protected by setting the access rights to read-only so that the files cannot be altered. Individual documents can have passwords set on them so that only authorised staff can open the file to read and/or edit the contents.

Figure 4.7 Protecting a document with a password

As well as protecting the whole document with a password, restrictions can be set on just parts of the document. This is useful in spreadsheets, where formulas must not be changed when an office worker is entering data. The data they are working on can be changed but the formula calculations must remain the same.

Figure 4.8 Protecting a cell in a spreadsheet

Anti-virus software

Anti-virus software is used to detect any viruses, including Trojans and worms and to remove them to limit their damage and impact to the computer system.

The software tries to detect the virus before it enters the computer system. If a virus is detected then the software will either automatically quarantine it or will send an alert to the user asking what action should be taken. Which of these actions the software carries out depends on the choices selected during the installation of the anti-virus software package.

It is important that the anti-virus software is kept up to date. When the package is bought and installed, it will be the most up-to-date version. New viruses are being created and distributed all the time, however, so the software manufacturer releases updates to reduce the risk from these new viruses.

Anti-virus scans can also be carried out by the package. These can be scheduled to automatically run at a selected time and day, or can be done by the user at any time. These scans will search for any viruses that may be on the computer system and that have not been detected by the anti-virus package.

Activity

Choose any two of the different providers of anti-virus software – look on the internet to see the different providers available.

Copy and complete this table to show the features that are available; two features have been given for you. You may need to add more rows to the table.

Consequence for safety	Provider 1	Provider 2
Internet links scanner		
Live support		

Encryption

However difficult access to computer files is made by using passwords and other means to keep out unauthorised users, data may still be copied or stolen. Encryption helps to prevent the data being used by unauthorised people.

Encryption software scrambles data when it is stored or transmitted between computers over networks.

Encryption software uses an **encryption code or key** to scramble (encrypt) the contents of data files. The proper code is needed to unscramble (decrypt) the file so it can be read and used as shown in Figure 4.9. If the encrypted file is accessed by anyone without the proper code to unscramble it, the data will be meaningless.

Key terms

Encryption software Software that is used to encrypt a file or data.

Encryption code/key A set of characters, a phrase or numbers that is used when encrypting or decrypting data or a file.

Digital signatures are an example of encryption and are used to check that a website or a message is authentic.

The data held by businesses about their customers and their financial details are encrypted when stored on physical storage media or in the cloud, so that if anyone steals the data the details cannot be used.

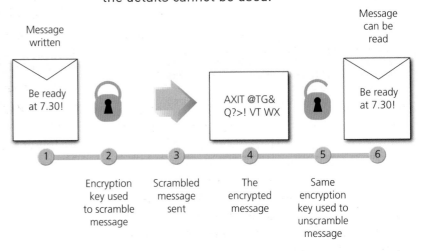

Figure 4.9 Using an encryption key to encrypt and decrypt a message

When customers buy goods or book cinema tickets online or when they enter personal details into any website, the data should be encrypted before being transmitted. This will keep the details from being read or used by others even if they are intercepted. Everyone should check that any website they enter personal details on uses encryption. A secure website using encryption will use https instead of http in the URL and will show a small padlock symbol. Different web browsers will show the use of https in different ways.

Figure 4.10 A website using encryption

Secure backup

A secure backup of data is a copy of data or files that are currently in use. Backups are made regularly and stored away from the computer system, preferably in another building in a secure place.

How often a backup is made will depend on what the data and files contain. A retailer will make back-up copies of its data and files every day, usually at a set time, after most of the day's work has been done. Banks and other financial institutions make backups every few minutes because their data is so important.

Top tip

When you are creating your project for R013 you will need to back up your data and work to make sure that nothing happens to it and that you do not lose your work and data. You will need to decide how often and how you will make a backup.

Businesses such as supermarkets have huge amounts of data, meaning that writable CDs or DVDs or USB memory sticks do not have enough capacity. Tape drives and extra hard disks are used to store the backups and archives of large companies. The tapes used in back-up tape systems have a large capacity but are expensive. Extra hard disks also have very large capacities but are not so expensive.

Backups created by businesses are kept safely so that they are protected from theft or fire. The data on the backups is often encrypted so that even if the backups are lost or stolen, no one will be able to understand the data without the encryption key.

Creating backups is so important that most large businesses are prepared to spend large sums of money to ensure they have adequate backups that can be used to recover any lost data.

The expense of using their own tape drives or additional hard disks can be too much for some businesses, so many use the cloud as an online backup, as shown in Figure 4.11. This means the backups are stored on servers managed by external companies, which charge for the service but take responsibility for providing the systems and for security of the data being backed up. The cost of these services can be much lower than paying for in-house IT technicians to manage and run back-up systems or for buying and maintaining dedicated back-up servers.

Top tip

You will need to keep up to date with emerging technologies that can be used as logical protection measures.

Practice questions

1 Describe **one** advantage and **one** disadvantage of using biometric prevention measures. [4 marks]

2 Discuss how access rights and permissions could be used to protect computer systems, files and folders. [10 marks]

3 Explain why a bank creates a backup of transactions every few minutes but a small shop creates a backup just once a day. [6 marks]

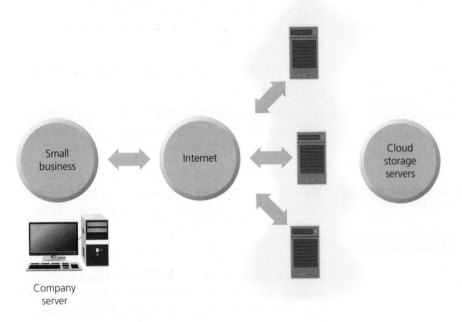

Figure 4.11 How cloud storage is used by a business for backup

Secure destruction of data

When data is no longer required, or it should be securely destroyed for legal reasons. This is to make sure that no data falls into the wrong hands. Even if data is deleted using the operating system software, it can still be located and used from the physical device, for example a laptop's hard drive.

There are three main ways in which data can be securely destroyed. Which way is used will depend on what data is to be destroyed and the storage device.

Overwriting data

The data to be securely destroyed is written over. Software is used to overwrite the data with random, meaningless data. This meaningless data is usually binary, composed of 1s and 0s. Meaningless data is written to all areas of the storage device. This method is usually used with physical storage devices. When the data has been overwritten the storage device can be reused.

Magnetic wipe

This means that the magnetic field part of a storage device is removed. This makes all the data stored on the storage device unreadable. Using this method can also make the storage device unusable. This is because the wipe also removes all the basic commands stored on the storage device – and these are the commands that make the storage device operate.

Physical destruction

The most secure, but probably the most expensive, way to securely delete data is through the physical destruction of the storage device. The physical destruction of a storage device may mean that it is so thoroughly destroyed that the data cannot be recovered. One example of physical destruction is the use of a hard drive shredder that shreds hard drives, a bit like a paper shredder. Another method is to use a drill or hammer through the hard drive.

In 2017, a hard drive containing unpublished and unfinished novels by Terry Pratchett was destroyed after his death. The method of destruction was extreme: the hard drive was run over by a steamroller!

Figure 4.12 A destroyed hard drive

It is also important that any paper-based forms that contain personal or confidential data are securely destroyed. Paper-based forms can be securely destroyed by using a paper shredder to shred them so no information can be read, or by burning them.

Practice questions

1 Identify **two** different methods of securely destroying data. **[2 marks]**
2 Describe what is meant by the term 'magnetic wipe'. **[2 marks]**

4.5 Current relevant IT legislation, its implications and applications

Legal protection

The specification does not list the IT legislation that you should know about in detail. *Important: The details of each Act in this chapter were correct when this book was published. During your study for this course you must make sure that you know about and understand the most up-to-date versions of each of the Acts, including any changes or additional pieces of legislation that are relevant to IT.*

Most of the UK IT legislation relates to the protection of individuals, organisations, technological equipment, information and intellectual property.

The main IT legislation you need to be aware of is the:

- Data Protection Act 1998 (DPA)
- Copyright, Designs and Patents Act 1988 (CD&PA)
- Computer Misuse Act 1990 (CMA)
- Health and Safety at Work Act 1974 (H&S)
- Freedom of Information Act 2000 (FoI).

Data Protection Act 1998

The Data Protection Act 1998 (DPA) aims to protect the rights of the owners of data – the data subjects. It does not protect the data itself. See Table 4.3 for key terms related to the DPA.

The Act (law) sets out rules on how the data should be stored and processed. If the owners of the data think their data is being misused then the DPA can be used to complain and to claim compensation.

Storing data on computers makes it easier for that data to be accessed and used by the business, but it can also make the data more available to those who would misuse it.

The DPA tries to protect individuals by giving them rights to access any data about themselves stored by others and to try and make sure that the data is processed appropriately. Most people would prefer that their personal data is kept private and cannot be accessed or used by anyone.

The DPA gives everyone the right to know what data is stored about them on a business computer system and the right to see it. If someone feels that they are not being allowed to see their personal data, or feels that the data is not being processed properly, they can contact the Government Information Commissioner's Office and ask for help. The Information Commissioner's Office will investigate the matter and if necessary can take action against the business.

Table 4.3 Key terms related to the DPA

Term	Explanation
Personal data	Any information about a living individual, which might include both facts and opinions, that includes sufficient information to allow the individual to be identified. Facts would include name, address and date of birth. Other examples of facts about an individual could include qualifications gained, medical history and known allergies.
	Details that contain name and date of birth would be considered personal data, while statistics collected from a questionnaire completed anonymously, without any details such as name or address, would not.
Data subject	The person the data is being stored about.
Data user	The person who needs to access or use the data as part of their job.
Data controller	The person who needs to apply for permission to collect and store data. The data controller is often the person in charge of the business, but sometimes a different person who works in the business may have this responsibility.
	This person decides what data needs to be collected and what it will be used for and how.
Information commissioner	The person who enforces the Data Protection Act. This is the person organisations need to apply to in order to gain permission to collect and store personal data.

The DPA lays down eight principles about how personal data should be handled by anyone storing the data.

1 Personal data must be fairly and lawfully processed.

This means that personal data must not be collected by misleading the person into providing it and that the personal data collected can only be used lawfully.

2 Personal data must be processed for limited purposes.

This means that personal data must only be used for the purpose for which it was obtained. For instance, a person's email address collected so that a business can reply to enquiries must not be used, without the person's permission, for any other purpose, such as email marketing.

3 Personal data must be adequate, relevant and not excessive.

This means that personal data that is stored should be just enough for the task to be carried out, only relevant to the task, and not include other data. For example, a bank would need to hold a customer's name and address, but not any details of their qualifications.

4 Personal data must be accurate and up to date.

This means the person storing the data has a duty to ensure that any data they hold is accurate and free from errors. This is the principle that most people worry about, because inaccurate data stored, for example by their bank, can cause many difficulties. Most people who ask to see the data held about them are concerned that a business holds data that is not accurate and want to get it corrected.

5 Personal data must not be kept for longer than is necessary.

Data should be destroyed or deleted when it is no longer needed. This should be carried out to ensure that others cannot read or access it.

6 Personal data must be processed in line with the individual's rights.

This principle ensures that the person's data is processed so that their rights are respected.

7 Personal data must be kept secure.

Any stored data must be kept secure. The DPA ensures that businesses that hold data must take precautions against its loss, unauthorised access and damage. The Act does not define the measures that must be taken, but this principle means a business must take proper security measures to protect the data. For example, a business could set passwords, levels of access and use physical methods of protecting the data.

8   Personal data must not be transferred to other countries outside the European Economic Area that do not have adequate data protection.

Other countries around the world may not have the same level of data protection as the UK, so the Act states that personal data must not be sent to countries with lower levels of data protection than those in the UK.

Top tip

You may select, store and process data about people when you are completing your work for R013. You must make sure that you comply with as many of the principles of the DPA as possible.

 Activity

A dental practice holds records about its patients, including personal details.

Make a list of the types of data that the dentist could keep about its patients. Do not list the actual data but write down items, such as:

● name
● date of birth.

Copyright, Design and Patents Act 1988

You should know about the Copyright, Designs and Patents Act 1988 from your KS3 study.

This Act (law) makes it illegal to copy a work, for example a file, music or image, without permission from the owner or copyright holder. It is also illegal to make unauthorised copies of software. People and businesses that break this law risk having to pay a large fine.

There are three main ways in which this law is most commonly broken.

● Using software without the correct software licence

For example, if a piece of software has been bought by a business with a licence to install it on three PCs but the business then installs it on four PCs, they have broken this law.

● Downloading files from the internet

If text, images and other files are downloaded and used, then permission from the copyright holder must be obtained. The name of the copyright holder should also be acknowledged. Sometimes the copyright holder may charge a fee for using their work.

● Copying music, DVDs, CDs and software

Any copying or sharing of digital files that you have not created yourself is a breach of copyright; copying and sharing MP3 files made from music CDs, and copying and sharing movies from DVDs, are all breaches of copyright. It is also illegal under this Act for a copy of a software CD to be made and installed on a PC.

Copyright lasts for many years after the initial publication of a work, but gives only limited protection to the person/people who created it. Owning the copyright to a piece of work does not stop others from copying it, it merely allows the owner to bring action in the courts. A problem is that often the person who copied the work cannot be traced. This is particularly a problem with computer software, images and other digital data, e.g. audio and video files, where copies are so easily made and shared.

Top tip

When you are completing your work for R013 you may need to find and use images or music. You will need to make sure that you follow the CD&P Act.

Computer Misuse Act 1990

This Act (law) aims to protect data and information that is held on computer systems.

The CMA relates to illegal access to files and data stored on computer systems. It was introduced to cope with the increase in hacking and viruses. There are three main parts to this Act.

● Unauthorised access to computer material

This means that any access to materials that you do not have permission to view is against this law, as is using a computer to access data or programs stored on another computer. This is often what people refer to as 'hacking'. Hacking is illegal only if you do not have permission to access the data or use the computer to access the data.

- Unauthorised access with intent to commit or facilitate the commission of further offences

Accessing computer material and then intending to use the information to commit further offences is against this law. This means that if you access information, even if you have permission to do so, with the intention of using it to commit fraud or blackmail, you are breaking this law.

- Unauthorised acts with intent to impair, or with recklessness as to impairing, operation of a computer

This means that any unauthorised alterations made to computer materials is against this law. So, if files or data are changed when you do not have permission, this is breaking this law. For instance, if you access someone else's computer files and change the contents, then you are breaking this law. Also, unauthorised altering of files to make the computer malfunction, to alter how it works or to damage other data also breaks this law – so sending a virus is a crime under this law.

Penalties for breaking this law can be a prison term of several years or a fine, or both.

Health and Safety at Work Act 1974

This Act (law) provides guidance to employers and employees when working with computer systems. The Act also defines actions that an employer should take to protect employees who work with computers in their job.

Almost everyone – not just all employees and employers – has a duty under the Health and Safety at Work Act (H&S) to work and behave safely. The Act also makes it illegal to act recklessly or intentionally to act in such a way as to endanger yourself or others. Employees must take reasonable care for their own and others' safety and must co-operate with their employers in doing so.

The Act applies to those using computers for their work but not necessarily to those using them at home, unless the employee works at home.

The main law covering the use of computer equipment is the Health and Safety (Display Screen Equipment) Regulations. These state that employers (a business) must do five main tasks to ensure the safety of their employees.

- Analyse workstations and assess and reduce risks

Employers need to check that the computer equipment and the area around it is safe. If any risks are found during the assessment of the workstation and surrounding area then action needs to be taken to make it safe.

- Ensure that workstations meet the minimum requirements

Employers need to make sure that adjustable chairs and suitable lighting are provided for employees. Tilt and swivel monitors should also be provided and the workstation should have sufficient space for the keyboard, monitor and any paperwork needed by the employee.

- Plan work so that there are breaks or changes of activity

Employees should not be expected to work at a computer all day. Regular breaks should be provided or a change in the activity that the employees are carrying out. The regulations do not say how long or how frequent the breaks should be, however.

- Arrange and pay for eye tests and glasses (if special ones are needed)

Employees of a business, who are covered by these regulations, can ask that eye tests are arranged and paid for. The eye tests can be repeated as advised by the optician – the business will have to keep paying for these. The business will only have to pay for the glasses if special ones are required.

- Provide health and safety training and information

Employers must provide training to make sure that employees can use their computer equipment and workstations correctly. This could include training on how employees can use the equipment to minimise risks to their health. The employees should also provide information to their employees about health and safety when using screen equipment (see Figure 4.13) and the steps that have been taken to minimise the risks.

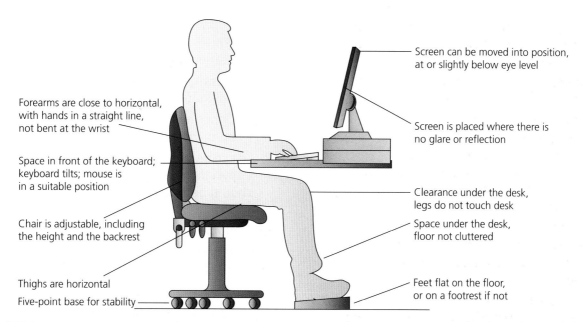

Screen can be moved into position, at or slightly below eye level

Forearms are close to horizontal, with hands in a straight line, not bent at the wrist

Screen is placed where there is no glare or reflection

Space in front of the keyboard; keyboard tilts; mouse is in a suitable position

Clearance under the desk, legs do not touch desk

Chair is adjustable, including the height and the backrest

Space under the desk, floor not cluttered

Thighs are horizontal

Feet flat on the floor, or on a footrest if not

Five-point base for stability

Figure 4.13 Correct and safe arrangement of a workstation

Activity

Investigate the Health and Safety policy, which applies to computer systems users, at your centre. Write down the main points of the policy and summarise how the policy affects the computer users.

Freedom of Information Act (2000)

The Freedom of Information (FoI) Act provides public access to information held by **public authorities**. It does this in two ways.

- Public authorities are obliged to publish certain information about their activities.
- Members of the public are entitled to request information from public authorities.

Key term

Public authorities Include government departments, the NHS, state schools and the police force.

The Act covers any recorded information held by a public authority. Recorded information includes any information that is held on printed documents, computer-based files, letters, emails, photographs and sound/video recordings.

The Act does not give people access to their own personal data (information held about them), such as credit reference files or health records. If someone wants to see their own data then they should make a subject access request under the DPA.

Anyone can make an FoI request to a public authority. It is the responsibility of the public authority to respond.

Top tip

You must ensure that you keep up to date with the developments in the legislation as the Acts can be updated or replaced by new laws. You should be able to apply the legislation to a given scenario.

Ethical and moral issues

With the increased use of computer systems to hold and share data and information, there are some ethical and moral issues that should always be considered.

The internet is a great place to share images, keep in touch with friends and family, and research information. Care should be taken, however, to make sure that information and equipment is not misused.

Another consideration when using the internet, for example, social media, is to avoid defamation of character. It is very easy, with the increased use of social media, to post comments that are not true. Defamation of character is when an untrue or false statement is made by one person about another. The statement tries to discredit a person's character or reputation.

This can also be known as trolling or cyber-bullying. You will have learned about cyber-bullying in your KS3 study. Trolling is when someone starts arguments or upsets people. This can be done by posting untruths or cynical/sarcastic comments. Some trolls specialise in posting untrue and false comments about celebrities, but this can just as easily happen to anyone. Trolls tend to think that, because they are using the internet, they can say or post anything.

Another consideration is that of libel. Libel is a written comment that is damaging to a person's reputation. Libellous comments can form part of trolling and cyber-bullying.

A good rule of thumb is that if you wouldn't say a comment to someone's face, then don't post it online.

Top tip

When you are selecting the data and information for R013, you should make sure that all information and data is accurate and up to date.

Practice questions

1 A business holds customer data.
   a Identify the Act that relates to the holding of personal data. [1 mark]
   b Describe **two** actions that should be taken to abide by this Act. [4 marks]
2 Describe **one** way in which the Copyright, Designs and Patents Act 1988 should be considered when selecting images for a website. [3 marks]
3 Explain what is meant by the term 'defamation of character'. [4 marks]

4.6 The importance of validity, reliability and bias when collecting and using data and information

Data and information can be collected from a range of sources, which can be classed as either primary or secondary.

Links to other sections

You learned about the sources you could use to collect data and information in Chapter 3, Section 3.3.

When data and information is being collected and used, there are three factors that need to be considered. These are validity, reliability and bias.

Validity

When data and information is being collected, how valid it is should be considered. 'Validity' means how believable the data and information collected is. For example, data and information that is found on a government, business (e.g. the BBC) or academic website would almost certainly be valid. Data and information that is found on a personal website may not be valid.

One example of non-valid data and information could be that of 'fake news'. Fake news is information that has been made up by those people who have written it. Many fake news articles were published during the US presidential election of 2016. These articles were mainly false but they were also unreliable and biased.

Activity

In May 2017, Facebook issued a guide to fake news and how to spot it.

Investigate this guide and evaluate the guidelines given.

Reliability

Data and information that is correct, and can be verified, is reliable. Incorrect data and information can be assumed to be wrong, out of date or inaccurate. Reliable data and information has a value, whereas the less reliable data and information is, the less valuable it is.

The reliability of data and information taken from secondary sources can sometimes be difficult to establish. If data and information is taken from a published source, for example a book, then the reliability factor will be high. This is because data and information found in a book will have been checked before it is published.

Care should be taken, however, when data and information are taken from newspapers and magazines. Do you think data and information taken from *The Times* newspaper will be more reliable than data and information taken from *The Sun*?

The reliability of data and information found on websites can be difficult to check. Anyone can set up a website and can post anything they want on it. Information found on the internet must be carefully checked.

The most reliable websites are those set up by official organisations and businesses. When data and information needs to be found on the internet then one way to check its reliability is to look at the website URL or address.

If the website URL ends with .gov, then the data and information it contains will have a high factor of reliability. This is because a website ending with .gov is managed by a UK Government department or council. Other website endings may indicate a high reliability factor or a low reliability factor.

Activity

Investigate websites that could be used as secondary sources for data and information. Complete the following table. The first row has been done for you.

Ending	Example	Example web URL	Reliability factor
.gov	A government department or council	www.ons.gov.uk	High, because this is the official website for the Office for National Statistics
.org			
.co.uk			
.com			
.sch.uk			

Reliability should also be considered when you are collecting your own data and information. The reliability of data and information collected from a primary source will depend on the collection method used, the type of questions asked, and who is asked to gather the data and information.

Top tip

When you are selecting data and information to use on your project for R013, you must make sure that it is reliable. If unreliable data and information is collected, then the computer system you are creating may not meet the defined needs.

Bias

Biased data and information gives only one point of view or perspective. When people write, they often introduce bias, either purposefully or accidentally. Information or data that is biased may be:

- a personal opinion
- a statement that does not contain any factual information
- prejudiced either for or against a person, product or idea.

For example, a music review website may contain biased opinions, because the person reviewing a track may or may not like the artist, or the genre of music. One review might say:

This is the best track ever from this artist.

There is no factual information in this sentence. How does the writer know that no track released by this artist in the future will be better than this one?

There are several ways to check the bias of information. For example:

- Look at who has an interest in a website. If a review of a product is on the manufacturer's own website, the likelihood of the review being biased is high.
- Consider whether the information is worded very simply, or very generalised.
- Consider whether the information seems to be based more on emotions or on facts and logic.
- Consider whether the information focuses on just one side of the discussion, for example being very negative or very positive.

Secondary sources can provide data and information that is biased. But biased data and information loses its value. When data and information has no value, it is of no use.

Top tip

When you are considering the validity, reliability and bias of any data and information you may select, you must consider:

- its source
- its agenda, or the point of view of its source
- its timeliness or how up to date it is
- its accuracy.

You will need to consider these factors on any data you collect and use on your project for R013.

Practice questions

1. Explain why it is important to consider reliability when collecting data. [3 marks]
2. Describe what is meant by the term 'bias'. [2 marks]

To be able to import and manipulate data to develop a solution to meet an identified need

About this chapter

Data-handling software can be used to create effective solutions. A client will require a customised product that meets their needs. Data handling can be carried out in spreadsheets and in database-management software.

In this chapter, you will learn how to select the most appropriate type of data-handling software and the tools and techniques to develop a data-handling solution.

You will learn how to import and link data and how to keep it secure. You will also learn how to use functions to manipulate your data.

Chapter content

5.1 How to create, edit, delete and process data using appropriate software tools and techniques

5.1 How to create, edit, delete and process data using appropriate software tools and techniques

How to create, edit and delete data using spreadsheet software

Spreadsheets have cells in which items of data such as values, labels, titles and formulas are stored. They are designed to handle numbers and to carry out calculations using functions and formulas. Spreadsheets can also create graphs to display or show trends in the data.

Top tip: spreadsheet software

It is very unlikely that you will use more than one 'make' of spreadsheet application in your project so make sure you know which application you are using, what its rules are and where to find help if you need it. Good places to start looking are the Apache OpenOffice Calc and Microsoft Office websites.

The spreadsheet examples in this chapter were created in Microsoft Excel. Other applications can be used but there may be some differences in their naming, keyboard shortcuts or rules.

In Calc, the entire file is called a 'spreadsheet', while in Excel it is called a 'workbook'. A single sheet within the file is called a 'sheet' in Calc and a 'worksheet' in Excel. 'Comments' in Excel are 'notes' in Calc.

An important difference is that Calc uses ; (a semi-colon) to separate arguments in formulas, but Excel uses , (a comma). For example, a formula using INDEX and MATCH, to do exactly the same task, would be =INDEX(D6:D9;MATCH(F12;E6:E9;0)) in Calc and =INDEX(D6:D9,MATCH(F12,E6:E9,0)) in Excel: the only difference is the character used to separate the arguments.

The examples given in this chapter should work in both Microsoft Excel and Apache OpenOffice Calc, but if you are not using Excel, you will have to ensure that, when you type in the formulas, you use the correct separator for the application you are using.

Cell referencing

Spreadsheet cells are arranged in a grid of rows and columns. Usually the columns are referenced with letters and the rows are referenced with numbers. Each cell has a unique reference based on its position in the grid, with the column letter first followed by the number of the row, as shown in Figure 5.1.

This cell is known as cell C3.

Other ways of referencing cells exist, but this is the usual method.

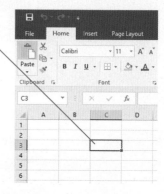

Figure 5.1 Cell referencing

When functions and formulas that use cell references are copied or moved, the spreadsheet will automatically update the cell references within to new values. This is called **relative cell referencing**.

Inserting a dollar sign ($) in front of the column and row references, e.g. $A$4, will stop the references being changed, so that the same cells are always referenced. This is called **absolute cell referencing**.

Key terms

Relative cell referencing Cell references change when the function or formula is copied or moved. For example, in =SUM(A1:D1) both the column and row references will change when copied.

Absolute cell referencing Cell references with a $ sign in front of the column and row references, for example =SUM($A$1:$D$1), do not change when the function or formula is copied or moved. Absolute referencing can also be applied only to the column, or only to the row; for example, =SUM($A1:$D1) keeps only the columns unchanged when copying, while =SUM(A$1:D$1) keeps only the rows unchanged.

The formula in cell C3 has been copied to D7 and the cell references in the formula have changed. It will not add up the correct range.

The formula in cell C9 has been copied to D10 but the cell references in the formula have not changed.

It will always add up the same range.

Figure 5.2 Absolute cell referencing

Functions carry out pre-set operations on data to produce a result. Spreadsheet software has many ready-made functions built in that can be used in **formulas** you create yourself.

Absolute cell referencing can be used with functions such as VLOOKUP, INDEX and MATCH to make sure that the correct **range** is always referenced if the function is copied to another cell.

> ### Key terms
>
> **Function** Spreadsheet functions are ready-made, built-in tools for manipulating data.
>
> **Formula** A spreadsheet formula carries out calculations on numbers using cell addresses and mathematical operators. It can use the ready-made functions.
>
> **Range** A group of cells in a spreadsheet that are identified by a cell reference. For example, the range of cells between, and including, A1 and D1 would be identified as A1:D1. Ranges can be named.

Arithmetic functions

Arithmetic functions do calculations. The arithmetic functions built into spreadsheets use arithmetic operators to carry out calculations.

Examples of these operators include adding up (addition), taking away (subtraction), multiplying (*) and dividing (/). Some examples of arithmetic functions are given below.

SUMPRODUCT
SUMPRODUCT is a very powerful function. In its simplest form it can be used to add up (**sum**) the results of multiplying the corresponding cells in two ranges.

> ### Key term
>
> **Sum** To add up.

For instance, a formula in cell C14 might be:

=SUMPRODUCT(C4:C11,D4:D11)

It works through the ranges C4 to C11 and D4 to D11, multiplying C4 by D4, then C5 by D5 and so on, to C11 and D11. Then it adds up the results of all the multiplications and shows the result in C14.

SUMPRODUCT is useful for analysing data. For example, Figure 5.3 shows the journeys of a group of taxi drivers who share cars.

	A	B	C	D	E	F	G	H	I	J
1										
2										
3										
4			Taxis	Driver		Journey		Cost per journey		
5										
6			A	David		5		£10.00		
7			C	Nigel		7		£12.00		
8			D	Mark		2		£9.00		
9			A	Rod		3		£11.00		
10			B	David		5		£7.00		
11			B	Kathryn		8		£10.00		
12			C	Jasmine		12		£8.00		
13			A	Kathryn		11		£12.00		
14										
15					Driver	Takings		Car	Takings	
16					David	£85.00		A	£215.00	
17					Jasmine	£96.00		B	£115.00	
18					Kathryn	£212.00		C	£180.00	
19					Mark	£18.00		D	£18.00	
20					Nigel	£84.00				
21					Rod	£33.00				
22										

Figure 5.3 The journeys of a group of taxi drivers who share cars

The formula in F18 is:

=SUMPRODUCT(($F$6:$F$13*$H$6:$H$13)
*($D$6:$D$13="Kathryn"))

The analysis could be used in a weekly report to show the takings of each driver and the takings from each car. Kathryn is one of the drivers and her takings can be extracted by the formula. The formula works by multiplying *only* the number of journeys in column F by the cost per journey in column H if the criterion 'Kathryn' is in the corresponding cell in column D. Similar formulas can be used to extract the takings of other drivers and of the cars.

Activity

Explain why the formula uses absolute referencing.

What is the formula in I16 in Figure 5.3 that calculates the takings from Car A?

ROUND, ROUNDUP and ROUNDDOWN

These functions are used to make numbers simpler while keeping each value as close as possible to the original value. For example, rounding 63 to the nearest 10 is 60, because 63 is nearer to 60 than to 70.

Numbers are rounded to make them easier to understand and because it's not always necessary to be exact. For example, checking a bill for a takeaway meal of pizzas can be easier if you round the numbers. If your bill has pizzas and items for £5.95, £0.99, £0.99, £3.74, £7.24, £11.66 and £12.25 then adding up the exact amounts will take time; if you round them to £6, £1, £1, £4, £7, £12 and £12, it is a lot easier and quicker to check, when collecting the pizzas, that the total bill is 'about right'. Rounding gives a total of £43 compared to the 'proper' total of £42.82, which is close enough when checking your change or in a hurry.

In spreadsheets, you can specify exactly how you want your numbers rounded. This is done using the formula:

=ROUND(reference,digits)

where 'reference' is the cell reference or the number to be rounded, and 'digits' is how many digits from the decimal place the number should be rounded to.

ROUND uses the normal rules and rounds numbers 1 to 4 down and 5 to 9 up. If the number of digits is set to 0 then it rounds to the nearest whole number (integer); if digits is set to less than 0 then the number rounds to the left of the decimal point; greater than 0 and the number rounds to the right of the decimal point. For example:

- =ROUND(1123.3467,1) produces 1123.3 because the number is rounded to the first digit *after* the decimal point.
- =ROUND(1123.3467,2) produces 1123.35 because the decimal part .346 is rounded to the second digit *after* the decimal point.
- =ROUND(1123.3567,-2) produces 1100 because the integer part 1123 is rounded to the second digit *before* the decimal point.

ROUNDUP and ROUNDDOWN are used to force the rounding. When you want numbers to be rounded up even in the range of 1 to 4, use ROUNDUP. ROUNDDOWN is used to round a number down even when it is in the range 5 to 9. For example:

- =ROUNDUP(1123.3467,1) produces 1123.4
- =ROUNDDOWN(1123.3467,2) produces 1123.34

By using these functions, you can control how rounding works in your spreadsheet.

Logical (Boolean) operators

These are used to compare values in calculations. There are three main logical operators:

- = is used to test if the first value is equal to the second, e.g. is X=Y ?
- > is used to test if the first value is greater than the second, e.g. is X>Y ?
- < is used to test if the first value is less than the second, e.g. is X<Y ?

Logical operators are called Boolean operators because there are only two possible results from each test: TRUE or FALSE.

Logical operators can be used in combination with each other, e.g. is X=<Y ? means 'Is X equal to or less than Y?'

There are three Boolean operators that can be used in formulas or when searching a database:

- AND will check for both conditions to be TRUE at the same time
- OR will check for one condition or the other, or for both conditions, to be TRUE
- NOT will exclude a condition from the results.

> **Top tip**
>
> Logical (Boolean) operators can be very confusing, so think out the comparisons that you wish to make before you write the expression – and test them very carefully.

Making decisions

The =IF() statement is used to make decisions. =IF() carries out a logical test and gives a TRUE or FALSE result. It is a very useful function as it can test more than one condition at a time, can be used with the logical operators and can be customised to display messages depending on the results of the logical tests.

The construction of the IF() statement is:

=IF(Logical test to be carried out, what to do if test is TRUE, what to do if test is FALSE)

The logical test must be able to return either TRUE or FALSE and the 'what do if test is...' can be customised to meet your needs. For example, if you want to give the result 'PASS' to test scores of 75 and over, and 'FAIL' to scores under 75, you could use the IF() statement:

=IF(A3>=75,"PASS","FAIL")

where A3 is the cell reference of the score being logically tested.

You must be careful to test your use of logical operators in =IF() statements to ensure that it does what you expect it to do.

Errors

Errors in formulas can produce unexpected results or display intelligible error messages to users when they are entering data. #DIV/0! or #N/A is not as easy for a user to understand as 'Please enter a suitable value' or 'Your value is not found in the range'. It is much neater to catch the error and display a 'friendly' message to a user.

The =IFERROR() function provides a way to catch errors and display your own messages, or to make the spreadsheet appear to ignore the error.

Most functions and calculations can be 'wrapped' in IFERROR() to control what happens if your formula produces an error.

If you require a user to enter a number in A1 that is then divided by the number in A2, all is well if the user enters a number in A1. If the user enters text or leaves it blank, however, then the result of A1/A2 is #VALUE or #DIV/0! Neither error message is very helpful to the user. If you 'wrap' the calculation in =IFERROR() like this:

=IFERROR(A1/A2,"Oops, you can't divide a number with that! Try again.")

then the errors will be trapped and will display your message if A2 contains anything other than a number. Your message must be enclosed with double quote marks.

Use an empty message if you want the cell to be blank when an error occurs:

=IFERROR(A1/A2,"")

In the example in Figure 5.4a, the price for two of the boxes has not been entered, so the 'Cost per 1 item' cannot be calculated and is showing an unhelpful error.

If the +IFERROR() function is used with a suitable message, then a much more friendly message is shown to explain what is wrong (Figure 5.4b).

	A	B	C	D	E	F	G
1							
2	Items	No. of items in 1 box		Price paid for the box		Cost per 1 item	
3							
4	Hats	120		£10.00		£0.08	
5	Pairs of gloves	100		£3.50		£0.04	
6	Shirts	20				#VALUE!	
7	Coats	1				#VALUE!	
8							
9							

Figure 5.4a An unhelpful error

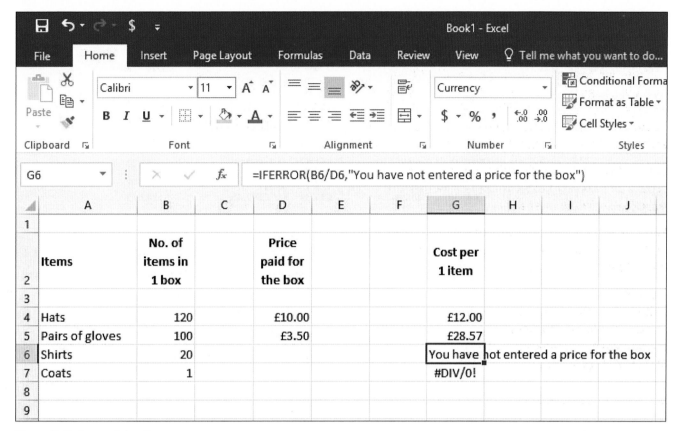

Figure 5.4b A user-friendly error message

LOOKUP functions

VLOOKUP

VLOOKUP is used to find a value in a table of data that corresponds to a value in the first column. VLOOKUP searches vertically down the first column until it finds the stated value, then looks across the columns for the wanted value.

The area (range) in the spreadsheet for VLOOKUP to look in must be stated. The stated value must be in the first column, column zero (0). The column to look in must be specified by counting across to the right from the first column, and the wanted value must be in that column. If either one of the values is missing, VLOOKUP will display an error.

VLOOKUP will only find the first stated value, but it can be set to find an approximate match rather than an exact match.

In the spreadsheet in Figure 5.5, VLOOKUP is used in G10 and J10 to find the name and profit made on the item code typed into cell F10.

The formula in cell J10 is:

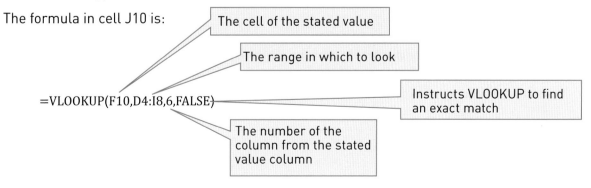

G17

Item code	Name	Purchase price	Selling price		Profit	
CH0032	Chair	£24.57	£45.00		£20.43	
TA8734	Table	£54.67	£96.50		£41.83	
CU8734	Cupboard	£124.76	£195.45		£70.69	
CA8636	Cabinet	£55.34	£102.45		£47.11	
Type in the code for the item:		CU8734	Cupboard		Profit:	70.69

Figure 5.5 Using VLOOKUP in G10 and J10 to find the name and profit made on the item code typed into cell F10

There is a similar formula in cell G10 to find the item name.

VLOOKUP could also be used to extract comments or grades for students depending on their examination results. A list of names and results could be analysed to decide on a grade using other functions, and VLOOKUP could be used to assign a comment or create a list of grades for a particular student, or a list of students with a particular grade (see Figure 5.6).

F3 =CONCATENATE(B3," ",VLOOKUP(D3,$B$13:$C$16,2,0))

Student	Exam mark	Grade	Comment
Terry	45	Merit	Terry has done well in this examination.
Andy	65	Merit	Andy has done well in this examination.
Rowena	79	Distinction	Rowena has done extremely well in this examination.
Roger	78	Distinction	Roger has done extremely well in this examination.
Carole	55	Merit	Carole has done well in this examination.
Mike	46	Merit	Mike has done well in this examination.
Chris	56	Merit	Chris has done well in this examination.
Brian	24	Not passed	Brian needs to retake the examination.

Grade	Comment
Not passed	needs to retake the examination.
Pass	has scored enough marks to pass the examination.
Merit	has done well in this examination.
Distinction	has done extremely well in this examination.

Figure 5.6 Using VLOOKUP with a list of student grades

In this example, the grade is assigned in column D from the exam mark in column E using IF statements. The formula in F3, replicated in F4 to F10, uses two functions: CONCATENATE and VLOOKUP. VLOOKUP looks at the grades in column D and extracts a suitable comment from the list, and then CONCATENATE joins it with the student name to create a comment about the grade.

Using item codes is not as easy as just typing in the name of the item, so, in the furniture shop example, it would be useful to type in 'Cupboard' and let the spreadsheet find the item code and the profit. Unfortunately, as the spreadsheet is set up, VLOOKUP cannot find the item code from the name. This is because the item code is in a column to the left of the name, and VLOOKUP only searches to the right. Functions MATCH and INDEX can be used instead.

MATCH and INDEX

MATCH can find where a value is so that INDEX can use the result of MATCH to find a corresponding value in a different list. MATCH can find 'Cupboard' and then INDEX can find its item code.

MATCH is used to find the position of a value in a list. So, if you want to find out the position of 'Cupboard' in the list from E5 to E8 in Figure 5.5, MATCH will find it for you. A suitable formula to find the location of 'Cupboard' using MATCH would be:

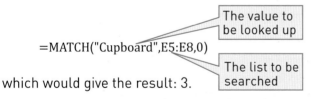

=MATCH("Cupboard",E5:E8,0)

The value to be looked up

The list to be searched

which would give the result: 3.

The result is the number of rows counting down; here it is three rows down from the top of the list.

The value shown by 0 in this formula decides what is to be found. All MATCH searches look for an exact match, but if this value is 0 (as in this formula) then the first match is found but the list does not have to be in any particular order; if this value is 1 the list must be in ascending order and the largest number that is less than or equal to the match is found; if this value is -1 the list must be in descending order and the smallest number that is or more than or equal to the match is

found. If this value is left out, then it is assumed to be 1.

Be very careful with these values. Using 1 instead of 0 in the formula produces the wrong item code because it finds the list is not in ascending order and the first value it finds is 'Chair' not 'Cupboard'.

A cell reference could be used instead of the actual value so that the user could type in the name of the item and MATCH could reference it and look up the position.

The position of an item is not much use on its own. INDEX can use the position to find a corresponding value in another list.

If the result from MATCH is 3, then a formula to find the Item Code of 'Cupboard' in the list from D5 to D8 is:

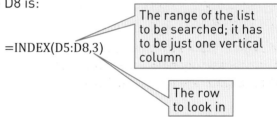

=INDEX(D5:D8,3)

The range of the list to be searched; it has to be just one vertical column

The row to look in

Like this, INDEX is not much use because you are actually telling it which row to look in – which means you already know where to look. Combining MATCH and INDEX will find the location and return the result you want. This formula will find the Item Code for the name of an item typed in cell F11 in the spreadsheet:

=INDEX(D5:D8,MATCH(F11,E5:E8,0))

In this formula, MATCH looks for the row of the value at F11 in the list E5:E8. The 0 tells MATCH that the list being searched is in no particular order. INDEX then looks down the list D5:D8 for the row of the value found by MATCH.

In the spreadsheet shown in Figure 5.7, the formula in G11 will show the item code when the name of the item is entered in F11.

Top tip

MATCH and INDEX can be very powerful search tools in a spreadsheet, but be sure to test them very carefully.

| G11 | | ⋮ | × | ✓ | *fx* | =INDEX(D5:D8,MATCH(F11,E5:E8,0)) | | | | | |

▲	A	B	C	D	E	F	G	H	I	J	K
1											
2											
3											
4				Item code	Name	Purchase price	Selling price		Profit		
5				CH0032	Chair	£24.57	£45.00		£20.43		
6				TA8734	Table	£54.67	£96.50		£41.83		
7				CU8734	Cupboard	£124.76	£195.45		£70.69		
8				CA8636	Cabinet	£55.34	£102.45		£47.11		
9											
10			Type in the code for the item:			CU8734	Cupboard		Profit:	70.69	
11			Type in the name of the item:			Cupboard	CU8734				
12											

Figure 5.7 Using INDEX and MATCH

INDIRECT

INDIRECT allows you to create cell references that change (are dynamic) instead of placing the actual references in your formulas. This means that you can change the references in the formula without altering the formula itself.

In D5 in Figure 5.8, =INDIRECT(F2,1) refers to the text in F2 and converts this to a reference to B2 where the value is 23. The value 23 is then shown in D5. The 1, which can be omitted, indicates TRUE, which means the text is a column/row reference. If FALSE or 0 is included, the reference is seen as a row/column reference.

INDIRECT can be useful when referring to ranges. A range called 'Cats' could be C2:C27, the text 'Cats' could be in cell G25 and, by using INDIRECT to reference G25, the whole range C2:C27 can be easily referenced from other cells. If the range 'Cats' is altered there is no need to alter the reference in the other cells. This can be used in data validation for constructing drop lists that are customised depending on the data entered.

D5		▼	⋮	×	✓	*fx*	=INDIRECT(F2,1)	

▲	A	B	C	D	E	F	G
1							
2		23				B2	
3							
4							
5				23			
6							

Figure 5.8 Using INDIRECT

Joining, splitting and presenting text

CONCATENATE

CONCATENATE is used to join the contents of cells without merging the cells themselves. It allows data to be kept separate and then joined as and when it is needed.

In the spreadsheet in Figure 5.9, a full customer name can be formed from separate lists of customers' first and last names. This is useful for reports when merging into other documents.

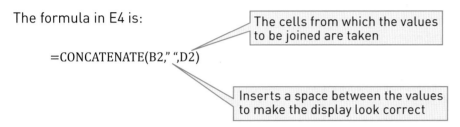

Figure 5.9 Using CONCATENATE

The formula in E4 is:

=CONCATENATE(B2," ",D2)

> The cells from which the values to be joined are taken

> Inserts a space between the values to make the display look correct

The result of using CONCATENATE is always text even if it is joining numbers. You cannot use ranges in CONCATENATE; each reference must be a single cell.

TEXTJOIN
TEXTJOIN is a new function found in the latest versions of Microsoft Excel.

TEXTJOIN is similar to CONCATENATE but it allows you to join a range of cells and to specify what goes between the values. The character between the values is called the delimiter.

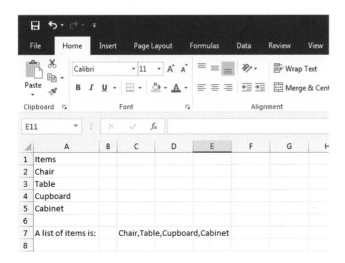

Figure 5.10 Using TEXTJOIN

The formula in C7 would produce the list as shown. Including TRUE allows the function to skip blank cells. If FALSE is used, the list would include any blank cells, which would appear as spaces in the list.

LEFT, RIGHT and MID
These functions are used to extract characters from strings of text.

- =LEFT("pineapple",3) will start on the left and return three characters, i.e. 'pin' is returned.
- =RIGHT("pineapple",3) will start on the right and return three characters, i.e. 'ple' is returned.
- =MID("pineapple",3,4) will start from the third character and return four characters. The first number is where to start, the second number is how many characters to return, so 'neap' is returned.

These functions are useful for manipulating data, such as converting date formats from mm/dd/yy to dd/mm/yy.

Email addresses can be automatically constructed from the names of people and companies using a combination of the above functions.

PROPER
This function turns the first letter of words into capitals and all the other letters into lower case.

Punctuation and numbers are not altered. It is useful for turning names into the 'proper' case, for example if cell B7 contained bRiaN gILLinder, this would become Brian Gillinder when referenced by =PROPER(B7)

This function can be useful when collecting a username from an input box in a user interface.

LOWER and UPPER

These functions convert text to lower or upper case. These functions can be useful when entering formulas. However, using the Text option on the Formulas tab in Microsoft Excel, the correct case of functions or data can be entered without having to check your typing.

DATE and TIME, TODAY and NOW

It is often useful to include dates and times in spreadsheets. Dates and times can be constructed and displayed using built-in functions.

=DATE(year,month,day)

=TIME(hour,minute,second)

can construct a date and time from cell references or numbers stored in your spreadsheet. This is useful when you have columns of years, months and so on, and want to create dates and times.

This can be used in conjunction with =TODAY() or =NOW(), for example to calculate how many days are left to complete tasks or with conditional formatting to highlight upcoming important dates in the next year.

Counting and adding data

COUNTIF

This function is used to count the number of cells that hold a specified value. If you wish to know how many cells hold a value in a given range of cells, then =COUNTIF(range,value) will tell you. The 'value' can be a reference to another cell and can use logical operators. Text can be used but must be enclosed in quotes.

SUMIF

SUMIF is used to add up (sum) any values in a range that meet criteria that you have specified. If you specify that you want to sum all the values in

a range that are larger than 10, then the function SUMIF will do that for you.

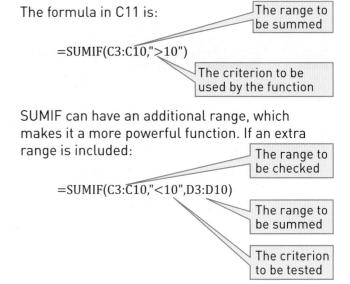

C11		× ✓ fx	=SUMIF(C3:C10,">10")	
	A	B	C	D	E
1					
2					
3			12		
4			9		
5			10		
6			11		
7			13		
8			15		
9			6		
10			16		
11		Total	67		

Figure 5.11a Using SUMIF

The formula in cell C11 uses the SUMIF function to sum the values in the range C3 to C10 that are over 10. It does not include the value in C5 because 10 is not over 10.

Activity

Rewrite the formula in C11 in Figure 5.11 to include values of 10 in the total shown in C11.

Rewrite the formula in C11 to sum values of 10 or less for the total shown in C11.

The formula in C11 is:

=SUMIF(C3:C10,">10")

The range to be summed

The criterion to be used by the function

SUMIF can have an additional range, which makes it a more powerful function. If an extra range is included:

=SUMIF(C3:C10,"<10",D3:D10)

The range to be checked

The range to be summed

The criterion to be tested

The cells in the range D3:D10 will be summed if the corresponding cells in the range C3:C10 meet the criteria <10.

D12			f_x	=SUMIF($C$3:$C$10,"<10",D3:D10)		
	A	B	C	D	E	F	G
1							
2							
3			12	0			
4			9	3			
5			10	5			
6			11	14			
7			13	6			
8			15	1			
9			6	0			
10			16	22			
11							
12			67	3			
13							

Figure 5.11b Using SUMIF with a range

The criterion to be tested can be a number, text, cell reference or another function. The criterion must be enclosed in quotes unless it is a single number.

Top tip

Make sure that you remember BODMAS when creating your formulas. BODMAS is an acronym for the order in which calculations are carried out.

- **B**rackets: Calculations inside brackets are always carried out first.
- **O**rders: Any numbers with powers or square roots are calculated next.
- **D**ivision and **M**ultiplication: These rank equally and are carried out as you come across them, from left to right.
- **A**ddition and **S**ubtraction: These are equal last in the order and are calculated as you come across them, from left to right.

Activity

Remembering BODMAS, what is the answer to this calculation?

$$(107+1004)-65+5^2+10*4$$

SUBTOTAL

The SUBTOTAL function is a very useful way to carry out calculations on a range of cells. It is especially useful when there is a lot of data and you want to pick out some of the cells and carry out calculations on them. Its syntax is

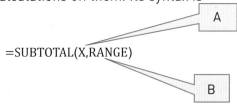

$$=SUBTOTAL(X,RANGE)$$

A is a number from 1 to 11 and specifies what calculation is to be carried out on the RANGE given in B. To add up (SUM) the values in the range, the number 9 is used, or to multiply (PRODUCT) all the numbers in the range, the number 6 is used.

Top tip

A list of the use of the numbers in SUBTOTAL is shown here:

- 1 AVERAGE
- 2 COUNT
- 3 COUNTA
- 4 MAX
- 5 MIN
- 6 PRODUCT
- 7 STDEV
- 8 STDEVP
- 9 SUM
- 10 VAR
- 11 VARP

It is worth taking the time to find out what each one does on a range of cells.

Manually hidden rows are not included in the calculations if you use the numbers 101 to 111 instead of 1 to 11 in SUBTOTAL.

Cells that are filtered out are never included in the calculations.

In the example in Figure 5.12, the numbers of boxes, rolls of tape and packets of labels have been added up using the SUBTOTAL function to pick out the ranges. Another SUBTOTAL function has been used to find out the average cost of a box.

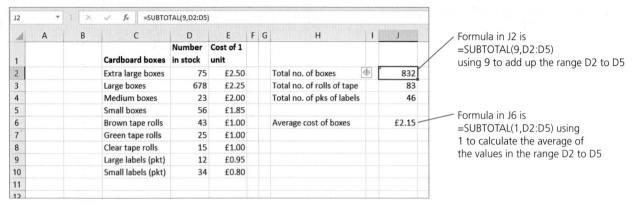

Formula in J2 is
=SUBTOTAL(9,D2:D5)
using 9 to add up the range D2 to D5

Formula in J6 is
=SUBTOTAL(1,D2:D5) using
1 to calculate the average of
the values in the range D2 to D5

Figure 5.12 Using SUBTOTAL

Linking worksheets

Functions and formulas can reference and use data in other worksheets. The name of the worksheet is included in the cell reference, for example =Sheet2!B11 is a reference to cell B11 in worksheet 2.

It helps if the sheets are renamed sensibly – for example =Customers!C17 – so you can easily see which sheet is referenced.

Linking to external data

External data can be linked to your spreadsheet so that you can use or analyse it.
A connection is made to the data using the Connections Wizard.

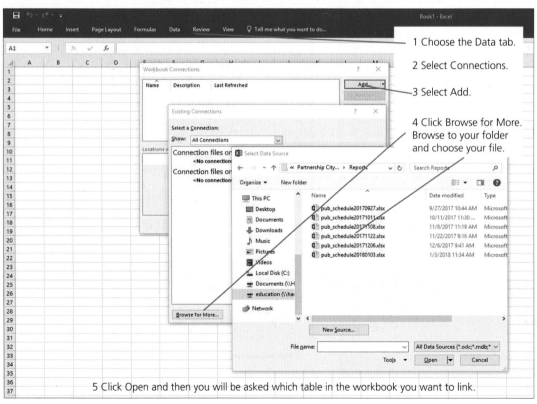

1 Choose the Data tab.

2 Select Connections.

3 Select Add.

4 Click Browse for More. Browse to your folder and choose your file.

5 Click Open and then you will be asked which table in the workbook you want to link.

Figure 5.13a Using the Connections Wizard

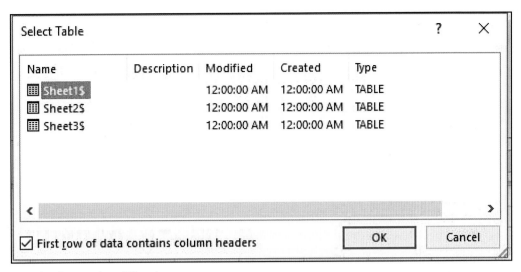

Figure 5.13b Using the Connections Wizard

To access the data, go to Existing Connections on the Data tab and follow the wizard to include the data you want and put it where you want.

The data can now be used as part of your spreadsheet.

Importing data

Data can be imported into an Excel spreadsheet from various sources. On the Data tab, the import wizards allow you to choose the most appropriate way to import your chosen data.

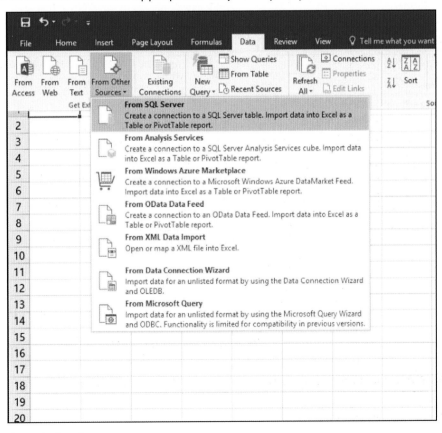

Figure 5.14 Using the import wizards

Usually, data has to be prepared before Excel will accept it. Data from other applications or from external sources is often sent to Excel as **text** or **CSV files**. CSV stands for Comma Separated Value (the **delimiter** for fields is a comma).

Key terms

Text file A plain text file. For importing into Excel, a text file uses tabs or spaces as delimiters for fields and carriage returns to separate records. A file using tabs may be called a TSV file.

CSV file A type of plain text file where the fields are separated by commas and the records are separated by carriage returns.

Delimiter A separator between values. The delimiter in this list of fruit is a comma: apples, pears, oranges. In this list of furniture, the delimiter is a semi-colon: chair; table; stool.

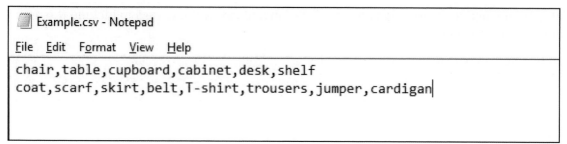

Figure 5.15 Data from a CSV file

In a text file, the delimiters can be spaces or tabs.

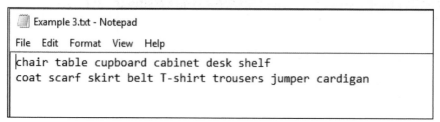

Figure 5.16 Data from a text file, with spaces and then with tabs

It is possible to use other characters as delimiters but care must be taken to avoid characters that appear in the items: T-shirt has a hyphen so using a hyphen here would cause the file to import incorrectly. Some avoidance of delimiter issues can be achieved by enclosing the items in quotes.

Both the text and CSV files can be imported using the Data / From Text option. Be sure to choose the Delimited options and to choose the appropriate delimiter for the file you are importing. A preview will show you what the file is using if you do not already know. A text file using spaces is imported as shown in Figure 5.17.

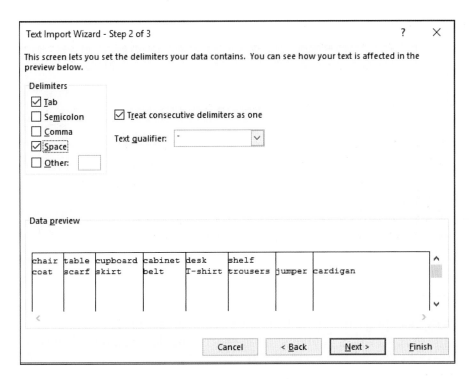

Figure 5.17 Importing a text file using spaces as delimiters

Presenting data

PivotCharts and Tables

PivotCharts are helpful when trying to make sense of data in a spreadsheet. In Excel, PivotCharts are created within the Insert tab. Blank columns or rows may cause an error when trying to do this.

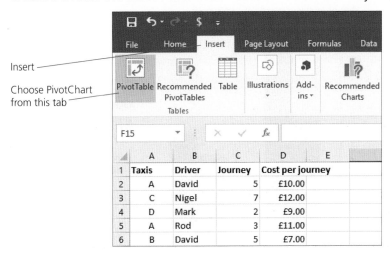

Figure 5.18 Creating a PivotChart

Inserting a PivotChart and choosing all the fields (columns) from the wizard will produce something like that shown in Figure 5.19.

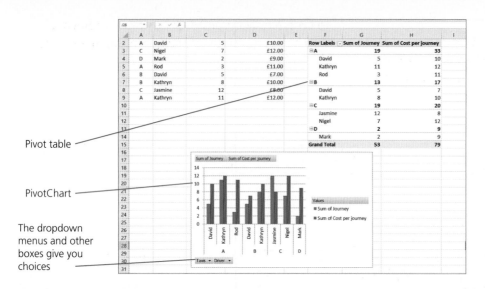

Pivot table

PivotChart

The dropdown menus and other boxes give you choices

Figure 5.19 Inserting a PivotChart

A PivotChart allows you analyse data by selecting the data to be shown at any time. For instance, by selecting the taxis and drivers from the drop-down box options in the charts, the data can be selectively analysed.

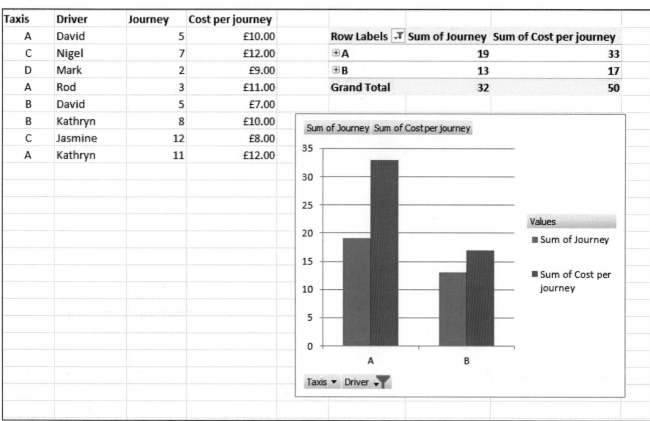

Taxis	Driver	Journey	Cost per journey
A	David	5	£10.00
C	Nigel	7	£12.00
D	Mark	2	£9.00
A	Rod	3	£11.00
B	David	5	£7.00
B	Kathryn	8	£10.00
C	Jasmine	12	£8.00
A	Kathryn	11	£12.00

Row Labels	Sum of Journey	Sum of Cost per journey
⊞A	19	33
⊞B	13	17
Grand Total	32	50

Figure 5.20 Analysing the data in a PivotChart

Inserting a PivotTable will create just the table and not the chart.

Dynamic charts

Dynamic charts update automatically as the data is changed. When rows and columns are added, the chart changes automatically to show the new data.

To create a dynamic chart, first highlight your data and turn it into a table from the Insert tab.

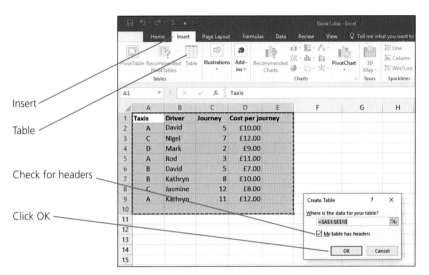

Insert

Table

Check for headers

Click OK

This set of data…

…becomes a table of data

Figure 5.21 Creating a dynamic chart

A chart created from the table of data will update immediately to show the amended data.

If you do not want to turn your data into a table, or you are using an early version of Excel, then you will have to use formulas. This is more complex.

Combination charts

It is sometimes useful to show your data with two or more types of charts at once. Combination charts can be used to show some data in a different way to other data.

To create a combination chart, first create a chart from your data then select a series of data in the chart; in the example in Figure 5.22 it is the journeys. The data for that series will be highlighted in the range.

In Figure 5.23, a line chart was chosen for the journeys.

Create a chart and select the series

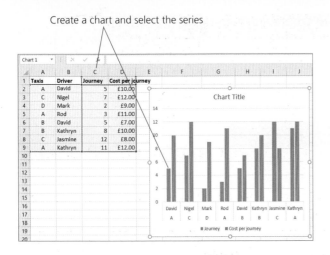

Click on Change
Chart Type

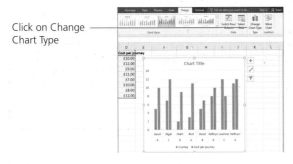

Figure 5.22 Creating a combination chart

Combination charts can be very useful for drawing attention to data within a range of data.

What-If Analysis

Spreadsheets can be used for analysing data and experimenting with it to answer questions about it.

What-If Analysis allows you to find what would happen to the results of any calculations if you changed some of the data. In Microsoft Excel, What-If questions can be answered using Goal Seek, as this sets a target and alters the data to achieve it.

In this simple example the profits are shown, along with the percentage mark-up on the purchase price. The seller would prefer all mark-ups to be over 40%.

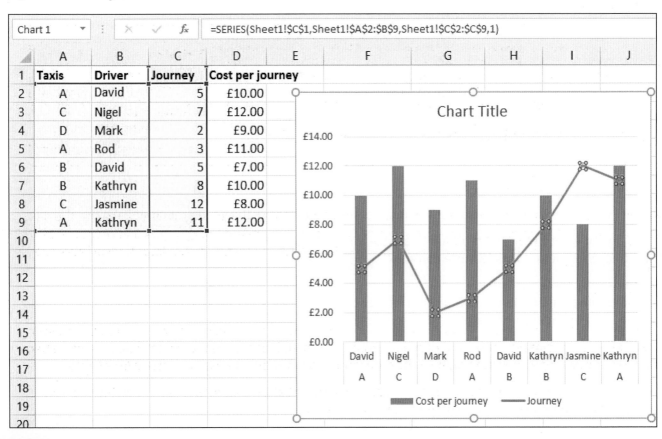

Figure 5.23 Adding a line chart

Item code	Name	Purchase price	Selling price	Profit	% mark-up
CH0032	Chair	£24.57	£45.00	£20.43	45.40%
TA8734	Table	£54.67	£96.50	£41.83	43.35%
CU8734	Cupboard	£124.76	£195.45	£70.69	36.17%
CA8636	Cabinet	£55.34	£102.45	£47.11	45.98%

A question to ask could be 'What should the selling price of the Cupboard be to make the mark-up over 40%?' What-If Analysis can answer this question.

In a spreadsheet, choose Goal Seek from What-If Analysis on the Data tab and enter the details into the box that appears.

Figure 5.24 Entering details in Goal Seek

In this example, the target was set to 41% (entered as .41), with the result that a selling price of £211.39 would be needed.

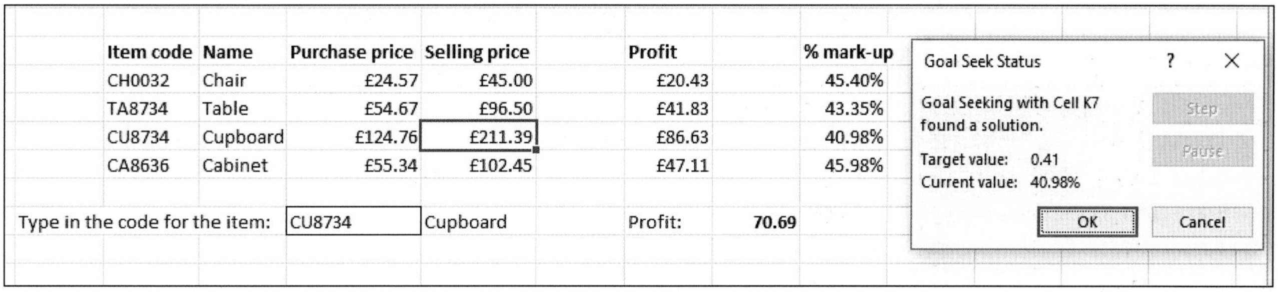

Figure 5.25 Using Goal Seek

Microsoft Excel provides a Scenario Manager, which allows you to make numerous changes to the data and to save these changes. Scenario Manager is then used to compare the changes and results side by side. You can switch between the sets of data to see the effects of changing the data. A PivotTable report can also be created.

Macros

Macros are used to automate tasks. Tasks that are repetitive or complex can be automated by recording, or writing, a macro that is activated by a button or command. Macros are stored as code in a worksheet and may or may not, depending on how they are set up, be available for use in other worksheets.

The simplest way to create a macro is to record the series of steps taken for a task, give the macro a name, and create and assign it to a button to make it work.

Sorting data can be repetitive so using a macro to sort a range a user has entered is a good way to speed up the sorting task.

To create a macro, choose the Developer tab and Record Macro. Give the macro a name and a description, if required, and assign a shortcut key combination if you wish. Then click OK.

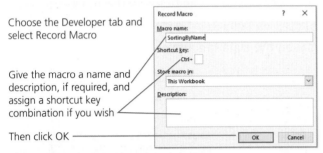

Choose the Developer tab and select Record Macro

Give the macro a name and description, if required, and assign a shortcut key combination if you wish

Then click OK

Figure 5.26 Recording a macro

All key strokes and all actions that you carry out will be recorded until you stop the recording by clicking on the button in the Developer tab, as shown in Figure 5.27.

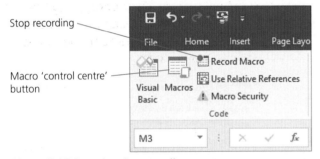

Stop recording

Macro 'control centre' button

Figure 5.27 Stopping the recording

> **Top tip**
>
> If the Developer tab is not shown, click on the File menu and then select Options from the drop-down menu. When the Excel Options window appears, click on the Customize Ribbon option on the left. Click on the Developer check box under the list of Main Tabs on the right. Then click on the OK button.

To create a new button in a worksheet, go to the Developer tab. Click Insert, Form Controls and choose Button

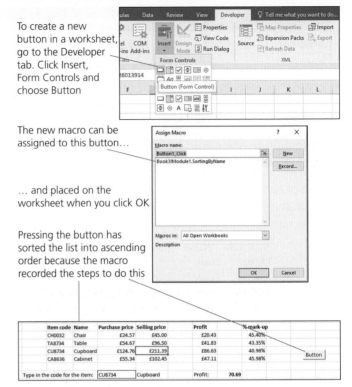

The new macro can be assigned to this button…

… and placed on the worksheet when you click OK

Pressing the button has sorted the list into ascending order because the macro recorded the steps to do this

Figure 5.28 Running the macro

The macro can be run by pressing the key combination, or from the Macros button in the Developer tab, or by assigning it to a new button in the worksheet.

The text on the button can be changed to something more suitable. When pressed, the button will carry out the assigned task by running the macro.

Macros are coded and stored within the worksheet. The code for the macro is assigned to the button, but it is far easier to record a macro than to write the code itself. The code for the macro can be seen by going to the option to edit the macro.

> **Top tip**
>
> Macros are very useful for tasks that have to be done regularly but with a choice of options. For example, if you use different printers with different settings for each, a macro will allow you to choose your required printer and options with the click of a single button.

Top tip

External objects can be embedded in a spreadsheet. Using macros to open an image or a document stored externally is useful. The object can be edited externally without altering the spreadsheet and the macro will continue to open the object and display the latest version.

Applying security

Spreadsheets can be protected in several ways.

In Microsoft Excel, a whole workbook can be protected, so that it will only open with the correct password. To do this, set a password using the Review: Protect Workbook option (see Figure 5.29a). The option to protect the Structure will prevent the workbook from opening at all, while the option to protect the Windows (only available in later versions of Excel) stops users closing, resizing, moving or hiding/unhiding a workbook window.

Individual worksheets can be protected with passwords, in many ways. The options are shown when the password is set and range from protecting selected individual cells to protecting the whole worksheet.

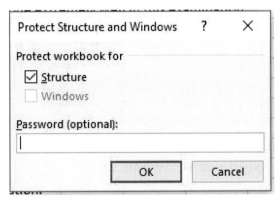

Figure 5.29a Protect Workbook

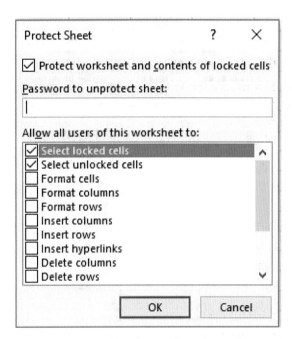

Figure 5.29b Protect Worksheet

Options to protect your spreadsheet include making the whole workbook read-only, so users can view it but not change it, or encrypting the whole file. All of these options can be accessed from the File, Info, Protect Workbook menus as well as from the Review tab.

Figure 5.30 Workbook permission options

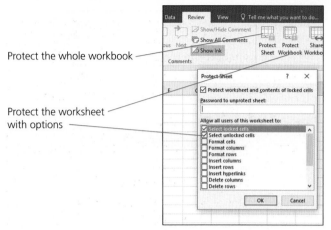

Figure 5.31 Applying security using the Review tab

Protect the whole workbook

Protect the worksheet with options

In Apache OpenOffice Calc, the options to protect your spreadsheet can be found under Tools, Protect document, where you can choose to protect the current sheet or the whole spreadsheet with a password.

Top tips

It is not possible to open your spreadsheet, or change it, if you forget your password, so make very sure that you can remember the password you used.

Do not password-protect your spreadsheets unnecessarily – and if you have to password protect a workbook or worksheet for your coursework, tell your teacher your password, or use 'password', so that an examiner can open your files to mark them.

Links to other sections

You learned about applying security in Chapter 4.

Exporting data

The data in your spreadsheet has to be exported or linked in order to be used in other software applications. A simple copy and paste may be enough to put the data into a word processor, but this will not work properly if you try to move the data into database software nor will it allow you analyse or update the data very easily.

Top tip

When pasting data copied from a spreadsheet into a word processor, try the special paste options to see which one suits your data.

Data can be exported as a text or CSV file, which can then be imported into other software. Text and CSV files retain the data but do not include any formatting or display options.

Linking, or embedding, data in word-processing software is preferred when the data is likely to be updated. As the data is updated in the spreadsheet, the update is automatically shown in the word-processed document.

To create a link to a spreadsheet in Word, use the Insert tab and choose Object in the text options. The spreadsheet will be embedded in the document. When the embedded object is double-clicked in the document, the spreadsheet is opened in Excel and can be edited. Any changes in the spreadsheet will automatically show in the Word document.

Top tip

Rows and columns can be hidden from view by using the Home / Format / Visibility / Hide/ Unhide options.

The complete workbook can be hidden from view using View / Hide. Unhide is there too.

How to create, edit and delete data using database software

Databases allow the entry, storage, editing, processing and retrieval of data. Companies use them to store details of their customers, clients, properties for sale or rent, stock details, and so on. Databases can be used to store almost any type of data.

Databases are created and managed in database-management software; the actual set or file of data is the database.

Databases are stored in files made up of records. A **record** is a collection of fields; each **field** holds one item of data about an object. Records and fields can be stored and displayed in **tables**. Figure 5.32 shows a set of records about furniture. Each row is a record about a piece of furniture. The columns are the fields with data about the item. For instance, the record for the 'Cupboard' is in the third row and has four fields of data about it: its item code, its name, what it is made of and its type.

Item Code ▾	Name ▾	Made of ▾	Type ▾
Ca8636	Cabinet	Wood	Oak
CH0032	Chair	Wood	Beech
Cu8734	Cupoard	Wood	Ash
Ta8734	Table	Wood	Canvas

Figure 5.32 A set of records

A database can be just one table of records (a flat-file database) or it may hold many tables of records that are connected together by relationships (a relational database). There should be a 'key field' in every record. A key field holds data that is unique so that each record can be identified from all other records. Relational databases separate data into tables, which allows the data to be accessed and arranged in many different ways without having to change the tables of data.

A relational database can have two or more tables of data linked together in different ways. The links are called relationships and are made between fields in the tables. The key field holding the unique data is a record called the 'primary key' and is usually, but not always, used to link the table to another table. A table receiving the link will have the same field in its records, but here it is called a 'foreign key'. A foreign key must be of the same data type as the primary key.

Key terms

Table Contains data about 'things', for example students, customers or orders. Each table has a unique name and contains data held in records.

Record A collection of data about a single item, such as a single student or customer. Each record must be unique.

Field An individual data item within a record. Each field has a unique name and contains a single data type.

Tables can be created manually and the data typed in, or the data can be imported from spreadsheets or other files. The relationships between database tables are then created.

A **data dictionary** describes how the database is to be structured. The data dictionary should have been prepared for any new database before construction of the database begins.

Relationships

A database of furniture items keeps records of the items in one table and records their costs in another. The link between the tables is the item's code number.

The data used to link tables must be unique and appear in both tables.

Figure 5.33 shows two tables from a database of furniture items.

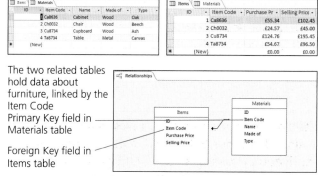

The two related tables hold data about furniture, linked by the Item Code Primary Key field in Materials table

Foreign Key field in Items table

Figure 5.33 Two tables from a database of furniture items

111

Relationships can be one of three types.

- *One to one*: Where both tables have only one record.
- *One to many*: Where the table with the primary key has only one record that relates to many records in the other.
- *Many to many*: Where each record in one table can relate to many records in the other. A third table is often needed in cases of many-to-many relationships.

Data validation techniques

A database is useful only if it contains data that is correct, reasonable and sensible. Data **validation** techniques can be used as the data is being entered to check that it is reasonable and sensible, but it is very difficult to check if the data is actually correct. Recording the colour of the sky at noon on sunny days requires that any data recorded is a type of colour. If the colour is recorded as grey instead of blue, the colour is sensible and reasonable – but it is wrong. The use of validation techniques in databases can check that the colour is sensible and reasonable but cannot check if it is correct.

Verification techniques can check for 'correctness' by comparing the data being entered into a computer system with the source from which it came.

> ### 🔑 Key terms
>
> **Validation** Checks that the data being entered into a computer system is sensible and reasonable. Validation checks the data against pre-set rules.
>
> **Verification** A check to see whether the data being entered into a computer system is identical to the source from which it came.

Table 5.1 shows some validation checks that can be used to make sure that data being entered is sensible and reasonable.

Table 5.1 Validation checks

Validation check	What it does	Example of when to use it
Presence check	Checks that there is some data in a field	When the field is a key field, as these cannot be left blank
Length check	Checks that the data has the specified number of characters	A UK telephone number must have 11 characters
Range check	Checks that the data has a number of characters within a specified range	A UK postcode has between five and eight characters
Lookup value	Provides a list of values for entry	When entering a person's title, Mr, Mrs, Ms, Dr, Prof could be provided in a list for the user to choose from
Format check	Makes sure that the format for the data is reasonable	A vehicle identification number is 17 characters long and has a set format that indicates where the car was built, what fuel it uses, the manufacturer, brand, engine size and type, a security code, the model and year and the vehicle serial number. Checking the format will help determine whether the VIN is valid or not
Input masks	Controls what is allowed to be entered into a field – used with a format check to set the format	When entering a UK mobile phone number, it can dictate that the number be entered as + country code, (0) followed by four numbers, a space, three numbers, a space, and a final three numbers

More than one validation technique can be used on a field. It may be necessary to insist that a field contains a car vehicle identification number, which must be in a specified format. In Microsoft Access, most validation can be set using the wizards provided.

In Figure 5.34, two validation checks are used on the Item Code field to ensure that a sensible item code of two letters followed by four characters is used. If the entry is missed out or there is format error, a message will be displayed.

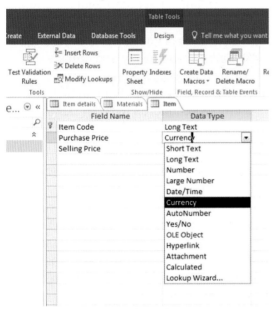

In Design View, you can set the data type for the field from the dropdown menu

You can set validation rules that require the field to have data, and display a message if no data is entered

Other aspects of the field can be set as required

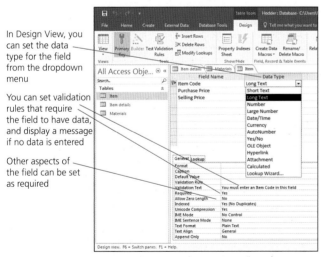

Figure 5.34 Two validation checks on the Item Code field

Top tip

Customise your error messages from validation checks to make them user-friendly and to help users.

Boolean operators such as = < > can be used in validation techniques. For example, a range check, e.g. >1 AND <100, will set a range to restrict the entry of numbers.

Activity

Input masks are a form of validation technique. Search the Microsoft Support for Office website to find the characters that you can use to define input masks in Access databases.

Input forms

Inputting data into tables in Access is made easier if a form is used. Forms can help the user by providing instructions and guidance as to what data is required and how to enter it. Warning messages can be used to tell the user if the data is not acceptable or if vital data has been missed.

Simple input forms can be created from Create / Form in Access. The new form can be customised and developed to suit your needs.

In the Access Create tab in Figure 5.35, a new form for the Materials table has been created. When it is saved and opened, it can be used to edit and add new records. A record can be deleted from the Database Tools tab. Any edited or added records are automatically reflected in the corresponding table when the table is opened.

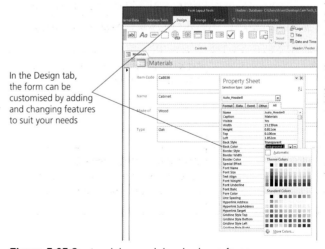

In the Design tab, the form can be customised by adding and changing features to suit your needs

Figure 5.35 Customising and developing a form

When creating a solution for a client, user-friendly and well-presented interfaces such as data entry forms will enhance the product. Forms can be used to enter data in more than one table by including the fields from the tables in your forms.

> **Top tip**
>
> When setting up your forms to enter data into more than one table, it is important to ensure that the tables are correctly linked. Incorrect links can cause input forms not to work as expected.

List boxes

A list box can be used to show a list of choices or values for a user to enter. A user can choose only from the list given; it is not possible to type any other value into a list box. List boxes can be resized to show more than one choice, or a scroll bar can be used to go through the choices. Combo boxes control how combinations of data are entered.

Check boxes

Check boxes are used to indicate responses to questions or comments on a form. The state – whether it is ticked (checked) or not – of the check box can be collected by the form and, when the form is submitted or saved, the data is entered into a field that can hold only one of two values: a Yes/No field.

> 🔑 **Key term**
>
> **Check boxes** These show a Yes/No choice – ticked when Yes, empty (clear or unticked) when No.

Check boxes have only two options – ticked or not – but many can be used in combination to indicate a range of choices. Tick boxes can be used to indicate the days of the week that a person is working: a tick box for each day would be yes/no but there would be seven boxes – one for each day.

Check boxes can be used to make data entry quick and easy for the user. It is simpler to tick boxes than to write lengthy responses.

Text fields

Text fields are used to hold text. The number of characters that a text field can hold can be changed if necessary. Text fields can be used to store formatted text in HTML or as Rich Text, but this will take up more space in the database.

Controls

Switchboards

A switchboard is a form that contains controls such as buttons to allow users to navigate around a database. Buttons can be set up to enable searching, create a report or move to different menus so that a user can easily and quickly find their way around the database. There is specialised software available that can be used to create excellent switchboards for your database. Often a switchboard is called a 'dashboard'.

Macros

Macros are used to automate tasks. Macros can be assigned to buttons that, when clicked, will carry out a task, or a set of tasks, that you have chosen. Opening a form or starting a report can be easily carried out with macros. While macros can be created by writing the code itself, they are more easily created using Macro Builder in the Design tab.

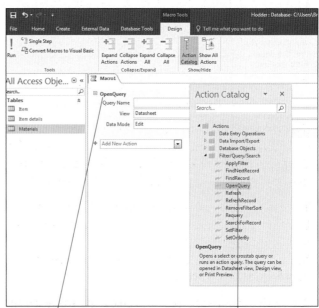

Clicking OpenQuery from the dropdown menu starts the macro building process by showing the sub-menus in the Action Catalog

A macro is being created to open a query using the Action Catalog

Figure 5.36 Creating a macro using Macro Builder

Querying a database

Queries

Queries are searches for data in the database. Questions are asked of the database and the data is collected from the tables. Queries are more powerful than simple searches because they can extract data from one or more tables and display the data in the way you chose when you designed the query. This makes it easier to analyse and understand your data.

Querying multiple tables at once is a powerful feature and allows complex questions to be asked of the database.

Creating a multiple-table query requires careful planning. The questions to be asked must be very clear, the data that you want to be included in the query results must be identified and the fields where it is to be found must be located. Then decide upon the criteria that you need for your questions.

 Key term

Query A way of interrogating and manipulating data within a database. A query has rules that filter to the specific data needed.

Deciding on the question for the query
The questions asked must be precise and clear if you are to extract the data that you want.

If a customer wants to buy a chair made of wood costing less than £200, the question to be asked of a database of furniture could be: 'Is there a chair, made of wood, that costs less than £200 in the database?'

The data that is needed to answer the question is located in an Items table and in a Materials table, so the query must look in these tables. These tables must be linked if the query is to be able to extract data from both.

A suitable query to find the data that answers the question would be set out as:

Chair AND Wood AND <£200

This would find only the records that met these criteria. The query needs to be in a form that the database can understand, but Access provides wizards to do this so you do not need to code the query yourself.

Crosstab
This is a way of summarising the results of a query in columns or a table so that they are easier to understand.

Wildcards
Wildcards in queries stand for unknown text characters and are useful when you want to extract data even if you are not sure how it is spelled, or you want to find data that does not quite match but is similar.

- * matches any number of text characters.
- ? matches any single letter.
- # matches any single numeric character.
- ! excludes characters placed in brackets.
- [] matches characters inside the brackets.

Criterion
This is the basis for a comparison. It sets out what is to be compared. In the question 'Is the chair made of wood?' the criterion is 'made of wood'.

Parameters
A parameter is a special kind of criterion. A parameter is asked for when a query is run. If you want to know how any items have been sold on a particular day, a query could prompt you to put in the day as a parameter when the query is run. Parameters are collected from the user with a dialog box that is set up when the query is designed.

Complex queries
Complex queries are used to extract data from multiple tables.

Query Design, on the Create tab, is used to select the tables needed for your query, as shown in Figure 5.37.

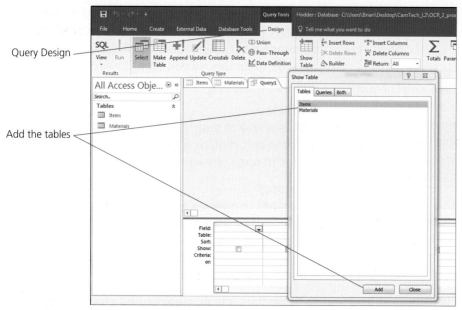

Query Design

Add the tables

Figure 5.37 Query Design

Choose the fields that you want to set up the query from the tables.

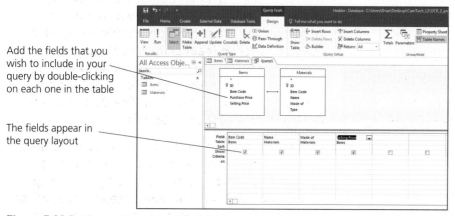

Add the fields that you wish to include in your query by double-clicking on each one in the table

The fields appear in the query layout

Figure 5.38 Setting up the query

When the query is saved and run, it will produce a table showing the results of your query.

The results of the query appear as a table

Figure 5.39 The results of the query

Calculations in queries

A query can show the results of a calculation carried out on other fields. Calculations are entered into the query in Design View, as shown in Figure 5.40.

A calculation to work out the profit is added (the purchase price subtracted from the selling price)

A new column called Profit is added in the results table, with the results of the calculation

The title of the new field is followed by a colon, then the names of the fields to be used for the calculation, in brackets

The results of the query, with the new column for Profit

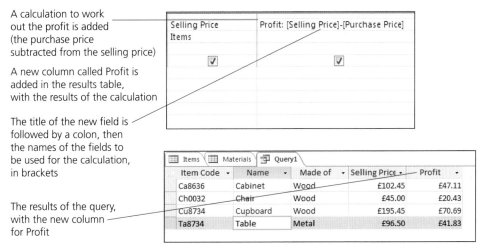

Figure 5.40 The results of a calculation carried out on other fields

Grouping information in Access

Queries can be used to group information in different ways.

- SUM will calculate the result of *adding* up a set of values. Fields to be added must contain numbers.
- MAX will show the *maximum* value in a set of values found by a query.
- MIN will show the *minimum* value in a set of values found by a query.
- AVG will calculate the *mean* (the total sum of the values divided by the number of items) of a set of values.

Database security

The whole database can be protected by a password. This protects the database by encrypting it so that a password is needed to open it.

It is difficult to protect individual tables and queries in later versions of Access, but they can be hidden from view. A well-designed user interface, such as a switchboard, will attempt to ensure that users do not look at individual table or query structures. One way to protect your tables is to have a separate file for the user interface section that can access the database files but prevents users from viewing or editing the actual files themselves. The navigation pane can also be hidden from view. The Database Tools tab contains an option to do this.

Different users can be given access to some areas of the database and restricted from accessing others. This can be accomplished by setting up tables of users linked to their access levels, which will send them to different navigation forms or switchboards.

Importing and exporting data

External data stored in text files and CSV files can be imported into a database in much the same way as importing it into a spreadsheet. Once imported, data is shown in a table.

Data is imported and exported to transfer data between software and to combine it with other data. Data can be exported from a database into a spreadsheet for analysis.

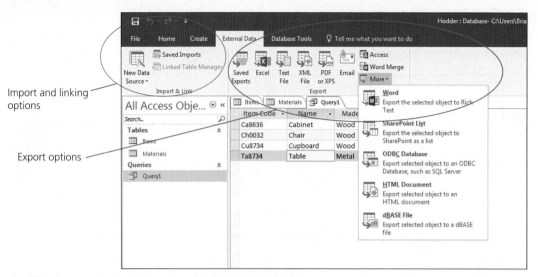

Figure 5.41 Importing, linking and exporting data in Access

Access has a whole section for dealing with importing and exporting external data in different formats to suit most needs. Data in a database can also be linked to external data in other software applications.

Linking a database to a web page or a presentation means that any changes in the data in the database will automatically show in the web page or presentation.

Often it is necessary to employ some coding techniques, or add-on software applications, on web pages in order to be able to dynamically use data from a database in web pages and presentations.

If you want to include data from your Access database in a web page, you must plan it carefully. You should create a 'data access web page' in HTML code. A data access page contains an 'Office Web Component' that stores the details of how to connect to your database.

LO6 Understand the different methods of processing data and presenting information

About this chapter

When data has been collected it needs to be processed. How it will be processed depends on the type of data and how it is to be presented. In this chapter, you will learn about the different tools and techniques that can be used to process data and the differences between the tools. Each tool and technique can be used for a different purpose, depending on the type of data that is to be processed.

You will learn about the different tools and techniques that can be used to present the information. The tools and techniques used may result from the format of the final results or may have been defined by the client during the initiation stage. Each tool and technique is best suited for different methods of presenting the information.

You will learn about the different methods that can be used to present the information. The information may be the result of the processing of the data. You will find out how different factors, such as target audience demographics

and availability of the information may have an influence on the presentation method selected.

What is important is that the presentation method selected enables the objectives that were defined in the initiation phase of the project life cycle. You will learn how to select a presentation method to meet these needs and how each presentation method is suitable for different purposes and types of information. You will learn about the advantages and disadvantages of each presentation method. By knowing these, you will be able to make an informed decision about the presentation method to be used and be able to justify your choice.

There are resources that are required to access and use the information. These are hardware, software and connectivity requirements. You will learn about each of these and how they may have an impact on the presentation method chosen and the distribution channel that is selected.

> **Chapter content**
>
> 6.1 Selection and justification of the appropriate software tools and techniques to process data to meet the defined objectives in a given context
>
> 6.2 Selection and justification of the appropriate tools and techniques to present information, including the purpose and suitability and the advantages and disadvantages
>
> 6.3 The resources required for presenting information

6.1 Selection and justification of the appropriate software tools and techniques to process data to meet the defined objectives in a given context

When data has been collected, it needs to be processed. The results of processing the data should meet the objectives that were defined during the initiation phase of the project life cycle.

> **Links to other sections**
>
> You learned about the phases of the project life cycle in Chapter 1, Section 1.1.

There are two main tools that can be used to process data. These are:

- spreadsheets
- databases.

Which tool is used will depend on the type of data being processed and the required results.

Spreadsheets

Spreadsheets are designed to store text and numerical data. However, a spreadsheet can also process and manipulate numerical data. The numerical data can be processed with the results being displayed visually in a graph or chart.

The format of the data used in a spreadsheet can be set to meet the defined objectives. For example, numerical data can be set as currency or percentage or to display a set number of decimal places. The format of the data will depend on the defined objectives for the processed data.

> **Links to other sections**
>
> You learned about the different data types in Chapter 3, Section 3.1.

Formulas and functions can be used in a spreadsheet when data is being processed and can instantly recalculate the results. If the figures inside a cell are changed, then any function or formula that uses that cell automatically recalculates and provides an updated result.

> **Links to other sections**
>
> You learned about some of the different formulas and functions in Chapter 5, Section 5.1.

Formula view can also be shown, using Formulas/Show Formulas, if any formulas need to be checked. Figure 6.1 shows part of a worksheet and the formula view.

Modelling can also be carried out using a spreadsheet; this can be known as What-If Analysis. What-If Analysis can be used to answer questions. Questions should have two parts: the change and the question. For example, if a shop takes on two extra employees (the change), how much more profit does the shop have to make to afford them? (the question).

	A	B	C	D	E	F
14						
15	Totals	£72,318.08	£64,258.08	£69,318.08	£86,891.08	
16	Net	£63,146.61	£55,086.61	£60,146.61	£77,719.61	
17						
18	Overheads					
19		Month	Annual			
20	Wages	4250	51000			
21	Rent	2800	33600			
22	Phone	127.78	1533.36			
23	Rates	1370	16440			
24	Heating	400	4800			
25	Totals	£8,947.78	107373.36	Inflation	10.00%	
26				Inflation Total	£894.78	
27	Charge per	£9,171.47				
28						

	A	B	C	D	E
14					
15	Totals	=SUM(B1:B13)	=SUM(C1:C13)	=SUM(D1:D13)	=SUM(E1:E13)
16	Net	=B15-$B27	=C15-$B27	=D15-$B27	=E15-$B27
17					
18	Overheads				
19		Month	Annual		
20	Wages	4250	=B20*12		
21	Rent	2800	=B21*12		
22	Phone	127.78	=B22*12		
23	Rates	1370	=B23*12		
24	Heating	400	=B24*12		
25	Totals	=SUM(B20:B24)	=B25*12		
26					
27	Charge per Dentist	=C25/4			
28					

Figure 6.1 Part of a worksheet and the formula view

A spreadsheet can contain many worksheets. A worksheet is one spreadsheet contained within a workbook – a workbook is a collection of worksheets. A worksheet can be used to store and process data about one specific area. For example, a worksheet may be used to store and process data relating to a specific month. In this example, 12 worksheets, one for each month, would make up one workbook.

Absolute cell referencing can be used when a cell contains a figure that never, or rarely, changes. For example, a cell could contain the VAT rate, which is currently 20 per cent. This figure rarely changes so a formula could use, or reference, the contents of this cell.

Spreadsheets allow a user to search for and sort by specific items of data, but this is limited in scope. Graphs and charts can be created using a spreadsheet and enable the user to visualise the data in an easy-to-understand format.

The main disadvantage of using a spreadsheet is that the formulas have to be correct for the results of the processing to meet the defined objectives.

Databases

Databases are also used to store and process data and text. They allow the entry, storage, editing and processing of data. A database is typically used by a business to store details such as customer records or stock details.

A database is stored in a **table** or tables. A table is made up of records. A **record** is a collection of fields. A **field** holds one item of data. An item of data is made up of characters.

A database can be just one table of data (a flat-file database) or many tables of records connected together by relationships (a relational database).

Links to other sections

You learned about some of the different features of databases in Chapter 5, Section 5.1.

A database can be used to store large amounts of data and text, as in a spreadsheet, but a database has the additional functionality to create complex queries. These **queries** can be saved and used in the future.

A database allows **validation** to be set on different fields. For example, fields can be set to a range of data types such as date, time, currency or logic. Using this reduces the risk of the wrong format of data being input by the user.

Links to other sections

You learned about the different data types in Chapter 3, Section 3.1.

Other types of validation can be set on the fields within a record. For example, if a field must be filled in, then a presence check can be applied to that field. The database will alert the user if no data has been entered into this field.

Other validation techniques can include length checks, format checks, range checks and input masks.

A database allows forms to be created and used when the data is being input. Databases enable the results of queries to be presented as a report, where the data can be shown in a variety of formats. Figure 6.2 shows an excerpt from a club database with the form that has been created for data entry.

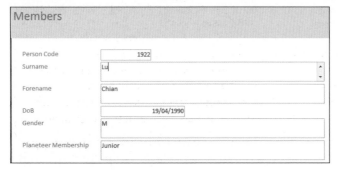

Figure 6.2 A form created for data entry

Links to other sections

You learned about the different data validation checks, forms and controls, queries and reports in Chapter 5, Section 5.1.

A database can help keep large numbers of records (data/information) organised, and the records can be saved for ongoing use. Input forms can be created and used to help in entering data with validation techniques.

Comparing databases with spreadsheets

Table 6.1 compares the advantages and disadvantages of using spreadsheets and databases, and gives examples of how they are used.

Table 6.1 Advantages and disadvantages of spreadsheets and databases

	Spreadsheets	Databases
Advantages	Formulas can be used to calculate and re-calculate totals What-If investigations can be carried out Modelling can be carried out Worksheets can be used to separate different sets of data in a workbook Data can be presented in a graph to make spotting trends and patterns easier Data types can be chosen to match the data being stored and processed Columns and rows can be locked to maintain data integrity Absolute and relative referencing can be included Data can be formatted to meet the needs of the audience	Lots of data, in records, can be stored Data can be added or edited if changes are needed Data can be filtered or queried to find relevant results Data can be sorted on a specific field, e.g. date order A password can be used to maintain the security of the data stored in the database Can be used with other software, for example to send personalised letters Validation can be set on fields to minimise input errors Reports can be generated to show the results of queries
Advantages of both	Can be imported into other documents, e.g. a presentation or report Can be saved and backed up to prevent loss or damage Can be shared electronically	
Disadvantages	If a model is created, the results may not be realistic Spreadsheet may take a long time to create Inexperienced users may struggle with the functions and formulae needed An error in a formula can affect the results Text cannot be manipulated easily	Knowledge and skill with databases are needed to set one up If more than one table is used, relationships need to be created If data from across many tables is required, queries can be difficult to formulate Security procedures need to be implemented if the database holds any personal details An error in data entry, validation or queries can affect the results

Table 6.1 (Continued)

	Spreadsheets	Databases
Disadvantages of both	If data is entered manually, errors may be introduced	
Examples of use	Calculating invoices Finding out the effect of a price change on sales of goods Producing a graph to show how many people used a shop for each hour that it was open Showing business accounts over a year, with each month in a different worksheet Importing data collected from, for example, a sensor or a survey Showing financial data with negative figures in red and positive figures in black	Holding personal data, e.g. about customers Sending personalised letters using mail merge Suggesting videos or products based on what a customer has watched, or bought, in the past Tracking stock levels in a supermarket Keeping track of all cars built by a car manufacturer, in case of any recalls, or keeping track of the service history of the cars Storing details of cars who have toll charge tags Keeping income tax records in the government

Top tip

In your exam for R012, you may be asked to select the most appropriate tools and techniques to process data for a given context.

Practice questions

1 For each of the following tasks, state whether a spreadsheet or a database would be most appropriate to use.

   a Calculating the total price of all goods shown on an invoice. [1 mark]

   b Storing the details of all members of a golf club. [1 mark]

   c Working out the monthly wages, with deductions for income tax and National Insurance, for the staff of an estate agency. [1 mark]

   d Storing details of houses for sale so they can be sorted into price order. [1 mark]

2 Explain why a database is the most appropriate software to use for storing and processing customer data. [4 marks]

6.2 Selection and justification of the appropriate tools and techniques to present information, including the purpose and suitability, and the advantages and disadvantages

When data has been stored and processed, the results have to be presented. Which tool is used to present the information will depend on:

● what information is to be presented

● how it is to be presented (which distribution channel)

● the objectives that were defined during the initiation phase of the project life cycle.

Links to other sections

You will learn more about distribution channels in Section 6.2 of this chapter.

There are five main tools that can be used to present information. Each tool has a different purpose, as shown in Table 6.2.

Table 6.2 Tools to present information

Tool	Purpose	Examples of what the tool can be used for
Word processor	To produce, edit and format documents that are mainly text-based	Writing documents, including letters, reports Mail merging
Spreadsheet	To store and process numerical data	Modelling and What-If Analysis Creating graphs/charts from the data stored in the spreadsheet Accounts A mail-merge source
Database	To store data and records in an organised way	Data handling Sorting data Searching for data and running queries Producing reports based on defined criteria A mail-merge source
Desktop publishing (DTP)	To arrange text and images into publications	Creating documents, including newsletters, flyers, posters, brochures
Presentation software	To create a slideshow to present information to an audience	Creating presentations to convey information

There are similarities between word processors and DTP. A word processor is generally used when the document being created is mainly text-based, while DTP would be more suitable to use when text and images are both to be used, as DTP provides greater flexibility on the layout of the text and images.

Each tool has advantages and disadvantages, as shown in Table 6.3.

Table 6.3 Advantages and disadvantages of each tool

Tool	Advantages	Disadvantages
Word processor	Easy to correct mistakes Documents can be saved and retrieved later Different versions of the same document can be saved Features such as borders and text layout can be used to enhance the presentation of the document Spelling and grammar checkers can be used to improve the quality of the document Document guides are available on how to lay out specific types of document Data can be imported from other files Mail merge can be used to create personalised documents	Files can sometimes become corrupted There may be a limited choice of symbols A device with word-processing software installed is needed to create documents
Spreadsheet	Can store and process numbers Can store text Numbers can be formatted to meet the defined objective, e.g. currency, percentage, decimal Complex calculations can be carried out What-If Analysis can be carried out Graphs and charts can be produced A wide range of formulas can be used Includes in-built functions	Inexperienced users can input incorrect formula If incorrect formulas are used then incorrect results can be shown Not able to process text-based inputs

Table 6.3 (Continued)

Tool	Advantages	Disadvantages
Database	Reports can be created to present results of queries Queries and reports automatically update when data is added Data can be stored in different tables, reducing duplication Large quantities of data can be searched more easily than in a spreadsheet	Can become complex if several tables are used Can be difficult to set up if the user is inexperienced An incorrect query can produce incorrect results Need to be kept up to date if the results of queries are to be relied on
Desktop publishing (DTP)	Frames can be used to position text and images in the document Drag and drop can be used to place images and other components in the desired places Text and graphics can be imported from different sources Software usually includes a range of templates so a novice user can quickly create a document Uses **WYSIWYG**	Different DTP softwares can have compatibility issues Can be difficult to create very precise layouts unless the user is experienced
Presentation software	Slides can include a range of different components, e.g. text, images, graphs A template can be used so all slides in a presentation look the same A slideshow can have links to other resources or files, e.g. a hyperlink to a web page The show can be presented by a speaker or automatically with no human involvement The message can be delivered to a large audience in a large space, without the need to print Automatic timings can be set for each slide or each element of a slide A speaker can decide when to move to the next slide based on audience involvement, allowing questions to be asked	Too much text on a slide can make the information difficult to read Effects such as animations or transitions between slides can become distracting Presentations may become unprofessional if too many features and effects are used

Key term

WYSIWYG What You See Is What You Get.

Activity

Find one more advantage and one more disadvantage for each of the tools shown in Table 6.3.

Practice questions

1 A sports club is producing a newsletter. Describe **two** advantages and **one** disadvantage of using DTP software to produce this newsletter. [6 marks]

2 A company wants to store and process stock records. Identify the most appropriate software for this task, justifying your choice. [5 marks]

3 A poster advertising a music event needs to be created. Compare the use of word-processing and DTP software for this task. [8 marks]

The purpose and suitability of methods of presenting information

There are several factors that must be considered when selecting the method of presenting information. These factors include:

- the target audience
- content limitations
- the availability of information
- the impact of distributing the information
- the distribution channel
- the presentation method.

Target audience

The audience the information is to be presented to, the target audience, needs to be considered when the method of presenting the information is being selected. If an incorrect or inappropriate presentation method is selected, the message of the information may not be understood.

There are several factors that should be considered when selecting the presentation method. These include:

- gender
- age
- ethnicity
- income
- location
- accessibility.

These factors are known as demographics. It can be very difficult to separate these demographic factors when the presentation method is being selected. The demographic of the target audience and the message of the information to be presented must be considered when selecting the presentation method.

The *gender* of the target audience should be considered. For example, some colours are considered to be 'male', 'female' or gender-neutral, so the colours used in a presentation to be shown at a meeting may need to be considered. Different audiences might respond to these colours in different ways. Remember that there could also be transgender individuals in the audience.

Activity

Investigate colours. Consider how different colours could be used to present information to different genders.

Age is very important when selecting a method to present information. Age groups could be classified as ranges, such as: 6–12, 12–18, 18–40, 40+ years. The method selected must be appropriate for the age group the information is targeted at. For example, if the message of the information relates to the launch of a new primary after-school club, then the audience may be children aged between 5 and 11 years old. It would not be appropriate to use a report to tell the children about the after-school club as a report would be mainly text-based. A presentation may be a more appropriate method for conveying this information.

The *ethnicity* of the target audience may need to be considered, as people of many different ethnic backgrounds live in the UK. Ethnic groups are found at a local level as well at a national and international level. One factor that may have to be considered is that of language. If the target audience is made up of a range of people from different ethnic backgrounds, then English may not be their first language. How the information is presented will need to take this into account. For example, if figures are to be presented, then a graph/chart or table may be easier to understand than trying to describe the figures using text. It may also be that a presentation could be used that will enable the information to be summarised, with a speaker providing further detail.

Another consideration may be the *income* of the target audience, in terms of the product or service that is the focus of the information being presented. For example, a website about second homes in the south of France is unlikely to be visited by people who work in low-paid jobs, as they will not have the disposable income to buy a second home. If the information relates to making meals on a budget, then a presentation, with printed hand-outs that the audience can take away for reference, may appeal to people who want to save money from their income or are struggling to make ends meet.

Where the information is being presented, the *location*, may also have an impact on how the information is to be presented. A report could be created to be distributed internally, for example to staff members, while a presentation could be created to be shown to people external to the business. The report and presentation could show the same information but in different formats. Another way of looking at location may be to categorise it into local, national and international.

Location is also related to the increased use of mobile devices. If the information is being presented over the internet, then the location of the devices used to access it can be very important. Parts of the UK have limited access to 3G or 4G services: this means that if the presentation method has a lot of content and will take a long time to download, people in those areas may not be able to access it on their mobile devices.

The *accessibility* of the information also needs to be considered. The information must be accessible to the target audience. This may result in the information being presented in a number of ways. A document could be created to be presented at a face-to-face meeting. If the information is then to be shared via the cloud, every person who needs to access the information must have access to the internet. If the information is a large file then a stable internet connection is needed.

Another definition of accessibility is accessibility to those people who have a disability. If a person has a sight problem, it may be difficult for them to read information that is presented in a text format. Solutions include providing the information in a large print or Braille format. Most websites offer accessibility options where text can be made larger or read out by a screen reader. If a person has a hearing problem they may not be able to hear music and sound effects in a presentation, video or multimedia product. It may be possible, with the aid of a signer, to interpret any spoken words to sign language.

Figure 6.3 Interpreting spoken words to sign language to increase accessibility

The information can be shared, or visible, in different ways. Information that is located on a website can be classed as *public-facing*. Another public-facing method may be that the information is shared in a face-to-face meeting, with an audience of one or more people, or using a presentation. Information can be shared using a *targeted* method This is where the information is provided to a specific range of people. This could be through the use of targeted emails or by responding to people who request the information through social media. Internal staff of a business could also have the information targeted at them.

Content limitations

Content limitations could also have an influence on the method selected for presenting information. It may be that the client has defined how the information is to be presented.

These limitations are likely to have been defined at the start of the project life cycle, during the initiation phase, when the user constraints were defined. For example, if the information relates to a business then a report and presentation may be identified as the methods to present the information. The content may also be defined in terms of the number of slides that can be used, if the information is to be presented using a presentation.

Other content limitations could include:

- the use of a pre-defined house style
- information, such as contact details, that must be included
- the use of any existing templates
- a word limit on a report.

Activity

Draw up a list of content limitations that could be defined if the information is to be presented at a face-to-face public meeting by a speaker using an on-screen presentation.

Links to other sections

You will learn more about the different presentation methods later in Section 6.2.

Availability of information

Real-time data

Information is all around us. It is available 24 hours a day and is constantly updated. There has been an increase in the availability of **real-time data (RTD)** over the past few years.

Key term

Real-time data (RTD) Data that is delivered immediately after it has been collected.

It is now possible on some websites to get RTD related to ships, flights and trains from all over the world. This enables people to have up-to-date and accurate details about departure and arrival times. Real-time journey details can also be provided on the ship, plane, train or bus.

This information can help people know what time they will arrive, for example at their destination train station. This could have an impact if someone needs to be at the station to collect them, as the arrival time will be updated in real time to reflect any delays. RTD can be used to help people plan their journeys and any connections that need to be made.

Figure 6.4 A real-time travel web page

Activity

Investigate the websites that provide RTD about ships, flights and trains. Make a list of the advantages and disadvantages of using these websites to find out RTD.

There has been an increase in the use of satellite navigation (satnav) systems in vehicles over the past five years. Some of the more advanced satnavs can:

- inform a driver of any delays on the planned route
- inform a driver of the length of the delay
- inform a driver of the cause of the delay
- offer the driver the option of planning an alternative route to avoid the delay.

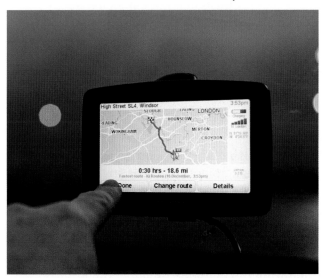

Figure 6.5 A real-time delay screen

These satnavs use RTD to be able to inform the driver. RTD can also be used on smart motorways to set speed limits based on the traffic conditions. The information given to the drivers on the motorways is available as soon as a delay occurs.

Figure 6.6 A speed limit on a smart motorway

It is now possible to get up-to-date weather information. Weather forecasts can predict where and when bad weather will hit. This can help prepare areas for bad weather, for example high winds, snow or storms. The ability to get RTD weather forecasts can help people prepare, but it can also track the progress of the weather.

 Activity

Investigate how real-time weather information helped warn parts of Texas, USA, to be prepared before Hurricane Harvey hit in August 2017.

Weather data can also help the emergency services prepare for the after-effects of the weather. In addition, coastguards, the RNLI and mountain rescue need to have up-to-date and accurate weather forecasts to enable them to carry out their rescues safely.

 Activity

Think about and research the impact of out-of-date weather forecasts on the emergency services including the RNLI, coastguard and mountain rescue. Discuss your findings with the rest of your class or in groups.

There has been an increase in the use of personal digital assistants over the last few years. These have increased the availability of real-time information for many people. These digital assistants are activated by voice and enable the user to:

- listen to music
- create, and add items to, 'to do' lists
- check a weather forecast
- learn first aid
- control smart devices in a house
- check, and add events to, a calendar.

When a question is asked, the assistant will get real-time information from the internet to provide the answer.

Figure 6.7 Amazon Alexa, a personal digital assistant

**Activity**

Investigate personal digital devices. Make a list of features and tasks that they can perform.

Location

The location of the person accessing the information is important. Most information can be accessed using the cloud. This, however, can have issues for some people. To access the cloud the user needs to have a connection to the internet. If a connection is not available or it is unstable then this may stop information stored in the cloud from being accessed.

Links to other sections

You learned about the cloud in Chapter 3, Section 3.4.

When the method that will be used to present the information is selected, the location of the information and the people who will be accessing it must be considered.

If the information is presented in a paper-based format, the only people who will be able to access the information are those who can physically access the report. This limits the accessibility of the information based on location.

Delays

RTD is very accessible due to the increased use of technology, so people have become used to accessing up-to-date information wherever and whenever they need it. Many people rely on having this information to enable them to do their jobs; for example, in the emergency services. People also rely on up-to-date information for their journeys, the weather and to keep informed about the latest world events

If the information is delayed in being released this can cause delays for people accessing and using it. It is also possible that any delay may mean that the information is out of date and consequently useless to the target audience. For example, a client may ask that information is collected and processed to be presented at a meeting. The deadline for this will have been set during the initiation phase of the project life cycle as part of the user constraints. If the information is not available on the day of the meeting then the meeting may have to be delayed and the information becomes useless. It is always important to keep to any deadlines that have been set by a client.

Links to other sections

You learned about the phases of the project life cycle, and the activities that are carried out in each phase, in Chapter 1, Sections 1.1, 1.2 and 1.3.

Another example of delays could be the information relating to traffic problems on a smart motorway. If an accident has occurred, then a delay in lowering the speed limit may result in long delays to drivers and could result in more accidents as drivers are unaware of the problem.

Activity

In pairs or threes, investigate how a delay in weather information could have an impact on people both here in the UK and internationally. Create a document and present your findings to the rest of your group.

The impact of distributing information

All information has an impact on the people who access and use it. Sometimes the impact of information can be made greater by how it is distributed. For example, if the information is to be distributed via a presentation, the impact could be increased by using sound, video and graphics as elements of the presentation.

Numbers can have a greater impact if they are shown in a graph/chart because the audience can visualise the numbers more easily. Diagrams can also increase the impact of any information. This is because, as with graphs/charts, people find it easier to understand diagrams rather than to read text.

How information is shared across distribution channels

When an information resource has been created, it needs to be shared with other users. One **distribution channel** is face to face – if the resource is to be shared at a meeting between two or many people, then face to face is the most suitable distribution method.

Key term

Distribution channels The methods that can be used to share information by individuals, organisations or businesses.

With the increased use of the internet and the cloud there are many different distribution channels that can be used to enable users to view, access and share resources.

How each distribution channel works is different, but each of them allows data and information to be shared, or distributed, between people.

Each distribution channel has advantages and disadvantages that should be considered when selecting the distribution channel.

Links to other sections

You will learn more about the advantages and disadvantages of different distribution channels later in Section 6.2.

Messaging services

Messaging services are one distribution channel that could be used. Messaging services include email, social media for business, and internal messaging channels.

Email is the abbreviation for electronic mail. Email provides a way in which a user can communicate with others. Email can be sent from a range of devices, such as laptops, tablets or smartphones, as long as there is a connection to the internet. Attachments can be sent, which can enable files – such as documents, videos and images – to be distributed between users.

Social media is a very popular distribution channel with businesses. 'Social media' is the term given to a dedicated website that allows members to interact with others. A business may have a page on social media that allows posts to be made, videos to be uploaded and members to react by posting comments, liking/disliking posts or sharing links about the business. A business can use its social media page to keep customers and other interested people up to date.

Many businesses have an internal messaging service. This is likely to be on the home page of the business intranet and can be used to keep staff informed, for example about any events or important information.

Activity

Your centre may use an internal messaging service. Investigate how this is used, the advantages and disadvantages of using this service and how access rights may have an impact on what information can be seen by users.

Websites

Websites are a very popular way of distributing information, and one method used for this is blogs. A blog is a regularly updated website or web page that is usually run by one person, the blogger, or by a very small group of people. The content of the blog is generally written in an informal style. A blog can be used to distribute information by the blogger writing about something. As with other internet-based distribution channels, information can be uploaded to a blog so the readers can either download it or read about it on the blog.

And here's Part 4 of my trip review. Part 1 was about holidaying with srprs.me. Part 2Part 2 was about holidaying alone and Part 3Part 3 was all about Malaga. This part is about travelling as a (lifelong) vegetarian.

This was by far the most challenging aspect of the trip and the single thing that concerns me most about doing another similar trip.

My first night, I ended up eating in the hotel bar, because I didn't feel confident about heading into the centre when it was dark and I hadn't yet found my bearings (would have been absolutely fine, especially with the help of the trusty maps on my phone, which got me around the city the rest of the time) and the restaurant had just shut.

Travelling while vegetarian

21 September 2017   Article   Life, Travel

Figure 6.8 A blog

Vlogs are like blogs in that one person usually runs them. The main difference between a blog and a vlog is that a blog is usually mainly text-based, while a vlog distributes the information through video. The videos can be downloaded to watch, or watched online. As with blogs, it is sometimes possible to download a text file that provides more information.

Intranet

An intranet is a private network that is accessible only to those people who have log-in, or access, details. An intranet can provide information to authorised users that is not available to those without access details. As a distribution channel, an intranet can be used if the information is to be kept to a small number of authorised people. An intranet could provide the platform for an internal messaging service. An intranet can also enable an internal website to be created and used by a

business. The web pages on the internal website can be used to distribute information, provide links to information or an internal blog, and allow files to be downloaded.

Internet

An internet website is one that can be accessed by anyone who is connected to the internet. Most businesses have a website and can distribute information through this website. A website can enable information to be posted directly or allow the information to be downloaded in the form of a file. A link to a blog or vlog can be given on a website that, when clicked, will take the user to the blog or vlog.

VoIP

VoIP is a system that enables voice calls to be made over the internet. A device or hardware is needed to convert the analogue signal made by the voice to digital to enable the voice to be transmitted. The devices being used to make and receive a VoIP call must have a NIC (network interface card) that provides the device with a MAC address and the means of communicating. This distribution channel is useful when information has to be 'talked through'. Files can be sent to the person accepting the call via email.

🔑 Key term

VoIP Voice over Internet Protocol.

VoIP can also be used with video calling using a webcam. There are programs that can be downloaded, usually for free, that allow calls to be made to anyone else who has the program installed. Some providers require a subscription to use the service, while others charge on a call-by-call basis. Examples of providers include Skype and Lync.

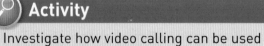

🔍 Activity

Investigate how video calling can be used by businesses and individuals. Present your findings to your group.

Multimedia

'Multimedia' is the term given to a collection of elements. These elements include text, sound, video and graphics. As a distribution channel, multimedia can be used to provide information in an informative yet entertaining way. Multimedia as a distribution channel can be very powerful and have a huge impact, but the elements must be carefully combined. Some multimedia can include user interaction, meaning that a user can interact with the multimedia to provide a personalised experience. For example, links to other sections of a site can be included so users can go to the sections they are interested in. Other user interactions can include being able to stop, pause, go back or forward.

Multimedia can be uploaded directly to sharing sites such as YouTube or can be embedded into a website or social media page. A website or social media page can also have links to the sharing site to directly access the multimedia.

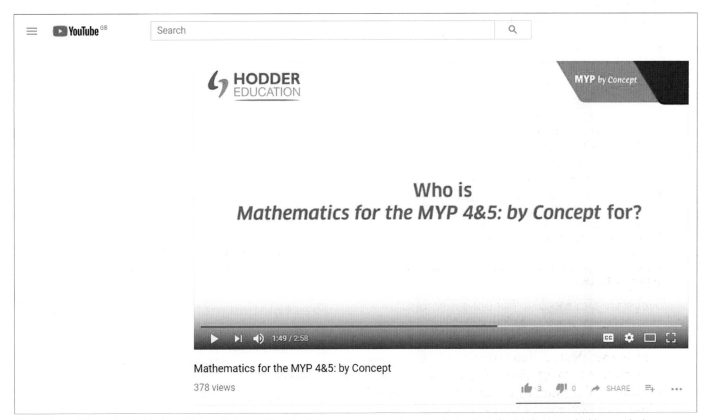

Figure 6.9 A video uploaded to YouTube. YouTube and the YouTube Logo are registered trademarks of Google Inc., used with permission.

Multimedia can be used as a distribution channel via a web conference. A web conference is when people who are remote from each other interact though speech via the internet. A webcam can be used so that the people taking part in the conference can see each other. During the conference, different documents can be seen and shared by all the people taking part in the conference. A web conference could be used as a distribution channel when people who are remote from each other need to access the information. A stable internet connection is needed, as is a webcam, speakers and microphone.

Cloud-based distribution methods

Cloud-based distribution methods are totally reliant on access to the internet. Documents can be stored in the cloud and can then be accessed by other people. Access rights may be required to access the information, which helps keep the information secure. The size of the files containing the information to be distributed must be considered. If the files are too large then they may take time to download or become corrupted during downloading.

Links to other sections

You learned about the cloud in Chapter 3, Section 3.4.

You will learn more about the resources needed to access information stored in the cloud in Section 6.3 of this chapter.

Mobile apps

Mobile apps are applications (apps) that are designed to be run on a mobile device such as a tablet or smartphone. Apps are available for many different purposes. They include fitness trackers, transport and travel apps and social media.

Figure 6.10 Apps on a smartphone

Apps, unlike websites, focus on one thing. For example, Transport for London (TfL) has several apps, each focused on a different part of the London transport network. One app checks the RTD of the bus network; another is a tube map app that not only shows the map but allows travellers to plan their journey.

There are apps that relate to people's lifestyles, and appliances that they own. NHS England has

created apps to help people track various aspects of their health, for example to help with healthy eating and work out how many calories in a meal. The cooker manufacturer AGA has an app that enables the owner to turn on their AGA remotely.

Activity

Investigate the apps available for a range of purposes. Look at the main purpose of each app, how it could be used by people, and the benefits of its use. Discuss your findings with the rest of your group.

Practice questions

1 Describe **one** advantage and **one** disadvantage of using multimedia as a distribution channel. [4 marks]
2 Explain the **two** effects to people that could occur as a result of a delay in the availability of weather information. [6 marks]
3 Describe how a targeted email could be used to distribute information. [4 marks]

Presentation methods

There are different methods for presenting data and information. Which method is selected and used will depend on the:

- defined objectives
- target audience
- distribution channel to be used.

There are six main methods of presenting information. These are:

- reports
- presentations
- graphs/charts
- tables
- integrated documents
- end-user documentation.

Each of these methods has advantages and disadvantages, as shown in Table 6.4.

Table 6.4 Advantages and disadvantages of each method

Method	Example	Advantages	Disadvantages
Report	Formal business report	Information about a topic can be collated and presented as a report Headings and subheadings can be used to enhance the structure of the report Graphs/charts can be included	If too much information is included then the user may not read the report thoroughly If the information does not 'flow' then the user may become confused The report must be checked for spelling and grammar errors – these can detract from the message of the report
Presentation	Presentation to customers or focus groups	Slides can include a range of different components, e.g. text, images, graphs A house style or template can be used Links to other resources or files, e.g. a hyperlink to a web page, can be included The show can be presented by a speaker or automatically with no human involvement Audience handouts can be created from the presentation	Too much text on a slide can make the information difficult to read Effects such as animations or transitions between slides can become distracting Presentations may become unprofessional if too many features and effects are used
Graphs/charts	Pivot, line, bar, pie, dynamic	Graphs/charts can help a user visualise the data better Titles and labels can be used to put the data into context Trends and patterns can be easily identified	A poorly presented graph/chart can cause users to misinterpret the data being shown If the wrong data is used to create the graph/chart then the data can become useless Using the wrong type of graph can make the information difficult to interpret
Tables	To show results	Information can be shown clearly and in an easy-to-understand format Good for summarising data and information	Headings must be used to indicate what each part of the table is showing Cannot provide full details
Integrated document	A document containing components from other documents	Components from other documents (e.g. spreadsheets or images) can be included to enhance the information in the report Graphs/charts can be included to enable users to visualise the information	Some software may be incompatible so components may not display correctly If too many components are used this can detract from the information in the document
End-user documentation	User guide or installation guide	Can help a user to use or install a product correctly Can include diagrams to show a user what to do Can be kept and referred to in case of any future problems	Must be written in easy-to-understand language If lots of text is used then the user may become confused Diagrams must be clear and fully labelled or they may be confusing

Links to other sections

You learned about graphs/charts in Chapter 5, Section 5.1.

You learned about presentation software earlier in Section 6.2.

You will learn more about the different features of presentations in Chapter 7, Section 7.2.

Practice questions

1 Information is going to be provided at a meeting with a speaker. Identify the most appropriate presentation method, justifying your choice. **[5 marks]**

2 The results of a survey need to be presented. Describe **two** advantages and **one** disadvantage of using a graph to present this information. **[6 marks]**

3 Explain the advantages to a customer of combining text and diagrams in a user guide. **[4 marks]**

Advantages and disadvantages of distribution channels

Different methods for presenting the information each have advantages and disadvantages. These must be considered along with the format or presentation method of the information.

Links to other sections

You learned about the advantages and disadvantages of different presentation methods earlier in Section 6.2.

Each distribution channel also has advantages and disadvantages. These should be considered when the distribution channel is being selected.

Links to other sections

You learned about the advantages and disadvantages of email in Chapter 3, Section 3.3.

Table 6.5 Advantages and disadvantages of each distribution channel

Channel	Examples	Advantages	Disadvantages
Messaging services	Email Social media for business (e.g. LinkedIn, iMessage, Twitter) Internal messaging service (e.g. Moodle)	A wide range of people can be sent or access the data/information The data/information can be targeted to specific groups of people Can be used as a marketing tool to gather feedback Files and images, etc., can be sent/uploaded	Security settings need to be considered Accounts can be hacked, leading to identity theft People can post inappropriate or offensive comments
Websites	Blogs Vlogs Intranet Internet	Can be used to get feedback Can be easy to update Alerts can be given when a new post/activity occurs Many people have access to the distribution channel	If not updated then data/information may be out of date The location of the data/information may have to be provided to enable people to access it
VoIP	Skype Lync Podcasts	Free if an internet connection is available Data/information can be sent at the same time as the VoIP call is taking place Features such as call forwarding, three-way calls, call waiting and voicemail can be used	If a stable internet connection is not available then the conversation may lag Each end of the call must have the right hardware and software to speak to one another The quality of the voice may not be good If there is a power cut then VoIP cannot be used

Table 6.5 (continued)

Channel	Examples	Advantages	Disadvantages
Multimedia	Web conference YouTube	The data/information can be shown or made available to one or many people Links to the multimedia can be embedded on Facebook/Twitter Different elements can be used – sound, text, video, animations Demonstrations can be included, e.g. to show how a product works As the multimedia is easy to change, it is flexible and can be used for many purposes	The message given through multimedia can be lost if too many elements are used If the quality of the multimedia is low, then the message may not be seen as reliable Too much information can be given If the users do not have the correct hardware/software then some elements may not work as intended
Cloud-based	Google Drive Office 365	Files are stored off-site so can be used as a backup Access rights can be given so documents can be shared Security can be implemented More cloud storage space can be bought when needed	Must have internet access to be able to download stored files The cloud provider has access to the data and information stored on their cloud storage area
Mobile apps	Travel Fitness	Features can be included in the data/information to increase user interaction Money can be raised if people have to pay for the app Apps can be linked to social media	Apps need to be constantly monitored and updated Regular maintenance needs to be carried out The app needs to be included on app stores or promoted so that people know about it

6.3 The resources required for presenting information

It is not only the method that needs to be carefully considered when data and information are to be presented. How the information is to be presented, where it is to be presented and the target audience all need to be considered when selecting the most appropriate presentation method. But, the resources required to use the presentation method are also very important. These include:

- hardware requirements
- software requirements
- connectivity requirements.

Hardware requirements

Differing presentation methods may require differing hardware. What hardware is required to view or use the resource will depend on how it is to be presented.

For example, if a report is to be used as the presentation method then no hardware will be required if the report is presented on paper (other than a printer). If the report is to be stored and accessed through the cloud, however, then some form of internet-connected device will be needed to enable a user to access and view the report.

Another example would be if the method selected is a face-to-face presentation. To view the presentation in this setting, a projector and screen would be needed, as well as the device the presentation is stored on. This may not cause a problem if the face-to-face presentation is to be shown in an office or conference room, as a projector and screen are standard equipment. If, however, it is to be shown in a village hall then the presenter may have to take their own projector and screen.

Figure 6.11 A projector is used for displaying presentations

Software requirements

The software that will be required should also be considered when the presentation method is being selected.

The software needed to use or view the resource will be depend on what the resource is. For example, if the resource is a report then the main software required to view or use it will probably be word-processing software. If the resource is an **integrated document** with components from other types of documents, however, then a greater range of software may be needed.

 Key term

Integrated document A document featuring components from other documents, including spreadsheets, databases or web links.

For example, a presentation resource has been created. Presentation software will be needed to view and use the resource. If the presentation includes links, however, for example to a spreadsheet or a website, then the software needed to view and use the resource will also include spreadsheet software or an internet browser.

It is possible to use a software that will allow the resource to be viewed across a range of devices and operating systems. For example, PDF creator/viewer software can be used to convert documents from word-processing software,

allowing them to be viewed on a range of devices. This may increase the number of people who can view the resource.

Some resources are presented using multimedia, for example on YouTube. To be able to view and use this type of resource, video-playing software will be needed. Some operating systems may have this included, but if not users may have to download and install the software before they can view and use the resource.

Activity

Fill in the table below to show the hardware and software that may be required when a resource is shared on different distribution channels.

Discuss your results with the rest of your class.

Distribution channel	Hardware	Software
VoIP		
Multimedia		
Mobile app		
Website		
The cloud		
Email		
Social media		

Connectivity requirements

The connectivity requirements to view and use a resource will depend on where it is to be viewed and used and which distribution channel is selected.

If a resource is to be stored online, for example in the cloud or on a website, then all the people who are to access the resource must have an internet connection to be able to access the resource.

One other consideration must be the size of the resource. If it is too big then it may take a long time for some users to download. There may also be an issue with **buffering**.

Key term

Buffering When an internet connection is too slow to show a resource in real time.

Practice questions

1 Explain how the presentation method may have an impact on the hardware required.

[4 marks]

2 Explain why a range of different software may be required to view an on-screen presentation. [4 marks]

Figure 6.12 Loading...

These issues must be considered when selecting the presentation method for a resource. If users experience issues with the size of the file, either with downloading or buffering, then they will be unable to access and use the resource.

To be able to select and present information in the development of the solution to meet an identified need

About this chapter

Solutions to problems can be presented in many ways.

In this chapter, you will learn how to select and use the most appropriate type of data for a given purpose.

You will also learn how to present the data, and the information derived from it, using the most appropriate software tools and techniques.

Chapter content

7.1 How to select and extract data for an identified need

7.2 How to present information using appropriate software tools and techniques

Top tip

You should make sure that you can use the tools and features in word processing, desktop-publishing and other presentation software so that you can make full use of them when creating your products and reports.

7.1 How to select and extract data for an identified need

To achieve high marks when presenting data, it is important to select data that is relevant to the project. Relevant data is data that applies to the situation and will help solve the problem.

The data that you need to collect should have been identified during the planning phases, when the methods of collecting data were decided upon.

It is important to select data that can be manipulated and presented in support of your solution.

The data that you have collected must be kept secure and be kept in accordance with any legal constraints.

7.2 How to present information using appropriate software tools and techniques

Different audiences and situations require different methods of presenting information.

Links to other sections
You learned about the advantages and disadvantages of different presentation methods in Chapter 6, Section 6.2.

Using word-processing and desktop-publishing software to present data

Table to text and text to table

Data that has been manipulated in spreadsheets and database software often appears in a table. If you want to present this data in a written document, it will sometimes be better to convert the table into plain text. There are tools available – for example via the Layout tab in Microsoft Word – to do the conversion, giving you a choice of separators that can then be removed using Find and Replace. In this way, you can change a table to plain text.

For instance, these tools can change a table of items such as this:

CA8636	Cabinet	£55.34	£102.45	£47.11	45.98%
CH0032	Chair	£24.57	£45.00	£20.43	45.40%
CU8734	Cupboard	£124.76	£195.45	£70.69	36.17%
TA8734	Table	£54.67	£96.50	£41.83	43.35%

...to this:

CA8636-Cabinet-£55.34-£102.45-£47.11-45.98%

CH0032-Chair-£24.57-£45.00-£20.43-45.40%

CU8734-Cupboard-£124.76-£195.45-£70.69-36.17%

TA8734-Table-£54.67-£96.50-£41.83-43.35%

...and, using Find and Replace, it can be altered for use in a printed document:

- CA8636, Cabinet, £55.34, £102.45, £47.11, 45.98%
- CH0032, Chair, £24.57, £45.00, £20.43, 45.40%
- CU8734, Cupboard, £124.76, £195.45, £70.69, 36.17%
- TA8734, Table, £54.67, £96.50, £41.83, 43.35%

Data can also be converted from a list of text into a table using the Insert / Table tab and choosing the Convert Text to Table option. The table can be copied directly into a spreadsheet, but there are better ways to import large quantities of data.

Links to other sections
You learned about importing data in Chapter 5, Section 5.1.

These tools are useful when choosing how to display and explain to different audiences the information you have extracted from your data.

Referencing tools

Footnotes and endnotes

A **footnote** is printed at the bottom of a page and contains extra information about the topic in the main text.

Endnotes have much the same purpose and layout as footnotes but all the notes appear at the end of a book or report. This is often more convenient than having many footnotes at the bottom of pages.

Footnotes and endnotes can be linked to the main text with numbers placed at the end of the sentence. It is not good practice to have more than one footnote or endnote attached to one sentence, but if you really must have more than one in a sentence, put the number on the most relevant word. After a footnote or endnote number at the end of a sentence, it is good practice to leave two spaces before starting the next sentence.

Key terms

Footnote An item at the bottom of a page with further information about the content on a page. Usually referenced with a number.

Endnote An item at the end of a book or report containing further information about the content in the text. Usually referenced with a number.

Footnotes and endnotes are both very useful for listing your sources of information to acknowledge where and from whom you got your information to avoid being accused of copying other people's work.

Footnotes and endnotes can also be used to add additional information or explanations that would seem out of place in the main text.

Captions

A **caption** is a brief note explaining a drawing, diagram or illustration. The title of the illustration could be the caption.

Key term

Caption The title or label of a diagram, drawing or photograph.

Content tables and indexes

Content tables are placed at the front of a book or report. They are used to show the chapters and the contents of the chapters in the order in which they appear.

Key term

Content table A list at the front of a book or report showing what is in the book or report.

Index An alphabetical list at the end of a book or report that helps readers to find items of content

Indexes are usually given at the end of a book or report and are used to help readers find important items. Indexes are given in alphabetical order to make it easier to find items.

Content tables and indexes can be created from the Reference tabs in Microsoft Word or from similar tools in other software applications.

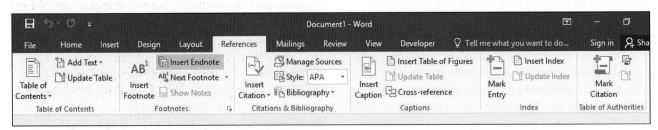

Figure 7.1 The References tab in Word 2016

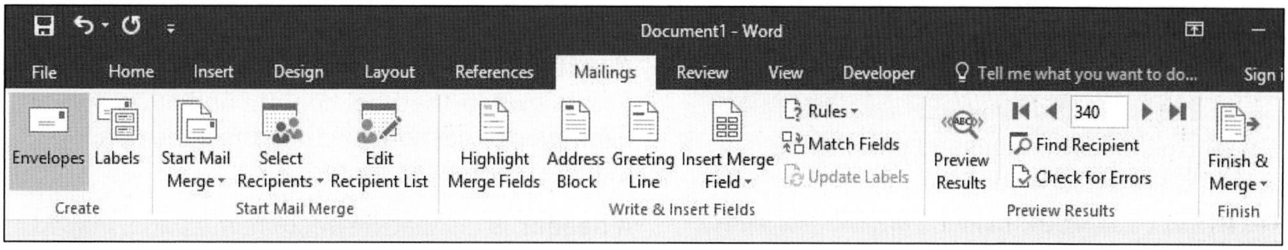

Figure 7.2 The Mailings tab in Word 2016

Mail merge

Mail merge can be used to create personalised documents that all have the same layout and formatting. Most sections of the documents remain the same but some sections are customised by including data from external sources. Sources can be spreadsheets, databases or text files.

When creating a mail merge, three documents are involved:

- the master (main) document
- the data source that will be used by linking it to the master document
- the merged document.

The data source must be carefully prepared so that the data it holds will merge properly. If the final, merged documents are to be letters and personalised addresses are to be included from a spreadsheet, then separate columns for the address lines must be created. Similarly, if the title, first and last names of the recipients are to be used, then it is usual to have these in separate columns. If a database is used, the items should be in separate fields.

The master document is created with the information that is going to be in all of the documents. It is laid out and formatted as required.

Merge fields are placed in the master document where the personalised items from the data source are to appear. Most word-processing applications have tools that simplify the mail-merge process. In Microsoft Word, the tools appear under the Mailings tab, as shown in Figure 7.2.

When the mail merge is started, the merge fields will take the required data from the data source and insert it in the position where the merge field appears.

Once the master document is fully prepared, it can be be saved. It is then available for the mail merge. It can be previewed for checking and then the mail merge can be carried out by printing or sending to email addresses.

Using macros to automate tasks

Links to other sections

You learned about using macros to automate tasks in Chapter 5, Section 5.1.

Macros can be created by recording the series of steps taken for a task, giving the macro a name and assigning it to a button or a keyboard shortcut to make it work. The button can be placed on the Ribbon in Microsoft Word ready to be used. The tools to create macros are found in the Developer tab. Macros can be used for tasks that you do often. Formatting text in a specific font, aligning text and spell checking can all be assigned to a macro.

Macros can be used to navigate documents. When using macros, it is important to plan what you are going to do with a macro. Plan the steps that you want the macro to carry out, where you want it to take the user and, if necessary, any messages that will be displayed. Try out and test the steps and when you are satisfied with your planning, record the macro. You can assign the macro to a shortcut or a button.

Linking and embedding data

Links to other sections

You learned about linking and embedding data in Chapter 5, Section 5.1.

External data can be included in your word-processed documents. This saves the time and effort of retyping all the data.

Data that is *linked* from other sources is automatically updated. If the data in a spreadsheet is updated, then the data in the document linked to the spreadsheet will also be updated. If the spreadsheet is moved, however, the link is broken. This makes it difficult to share documents that have linked data with other people because both the main document and the spreadsheet source have to be shared. Data must be edited and updated in the spreadsheet source since any changes made in the main document will not be made to the spreadsheet data.

Embedding data into a document is different from linking data to a document. Data that is embedded into a document is stored in the document and is not updated when the original data source is changed. You must update the embedded data yourself. Documents with embedded data are easier to distribute to others as all the data is in the document file. The file may be very big if there is a lot of embedded data.

Watermarks

Watermarks are patterns of light and dark shading that are used in documents and images. The pattern can be shapes or words and is used to identify the owner, put restrictions on the use of an image or to show that the document or image being printed is from a trial version of software. Buying a licence for the software removes the watermarks from future output.

Key term

Watermark A pattern printed or inserted across an image or document.

Sections, headers and footers

A **section** of page refers to an area of a page that has its own formatting, content and purpose. Examples of sections include the page headers, main text and page footers.

A **header** is a separate section of a page, placed above the main section of the text at the top of a page. Headers can contain any information that you wish – often they show the book or report title and the page number.

A **footer** is a separate section of a page, placed below the main section of the text at the bottom of a page. It often contains the page numbering and can contain footnotes. The size of a footer may be quite large if there are many footnotes to be included.

Headers and footers can be automatically duplicated on every page so can be used to display page numbers, logos, addresses or other useful information that might be wanted on every page.

Headers and footers can be created from the Insert tab or by double-clicking on the top or bottom area of a page to access the Header & Footer Tools.

Headers and footers can be included in a table of contents. First, ensure that all your headers and footers have a consistent style, then select your insertion point and use the tools to add them to your table. You do not need to include all the text of the header or footer in your table of contents.

Key terms

Section An area of a page that has its own formatting.

Header The section at the top of a page that contains information that appears on every page.

Footer The section at the bottom of a page that contains information that appears on every page.

Reviewing documents

All documents should be reviewed to make sure that they are as free from errors as possible. Several people usually review a new document and make comments or suggest changes. Word-processing and desktop-publishing applications provide tools for document review.

Documents are reviewed to check for spelling and grammar mistakes, that the content is correct, the titles, contents and indexes are complete and accurate, and that the document is consistently formatted throughout with accurate page numbering and layouts.

Making comments in a document

Comments can be added and appear with a line linking the comment to the point it refers to. Comments are useful for making suggestions or giving opinions without altering the document.

> ### 🔑 Key terms
>
> **Comment** A note attached to a piece of text.
>
> **Track Changes** A system of making changes to text but retaining the original text so that changes can be seen and, if required, reversed.

Tracking amendments to the document

Any changes made by reviewers can be saved and reversed if necessary. Most office software packages, including Microsoft Office, provide a variety of Track Changes tools to help when reviewing documents. Changes can be accepted or declined either one by one or over the whole document.

Making sure the document can be understood

Documents that cannot be understood are a waste of everyone's time. Your reports must be readable and make sense. Readability is one measure of how easy a document is to read and follow. People with poor or average reading comprehension need to put more effort into reading and understanding documents than those who have high reading comprehension. Your report should be worded carefully to make sure that everyone can read it easily. Flesch-Kincaid readability tests use the number of words, sentences and syllables to produce a score that can be used to assign a level of readability to a paragraph or document. Higher scores on a Flesch-Kincaid readability test mean that a document is easier to read than one with lower scores. There are also other readability tests, e.g. Dale–Chall, Fry and ATOS, that attempt to measure the readability of texts.

It is more difficult to alter the text in a document or in a report to make it easier to read after you have created it. Instead, start out by making your documents easy to read – if you can understand them easily when you read your work, then it is likely that others will be able to do so as well.

Document security

> ### Links to other sections
>
> You learned about document security in Chapter 5, Section 5.1.

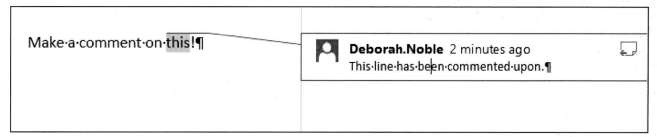

Figure 7.3 A comment in a Word document

A password can be placed on a whole document to restrict access. A password can be required to open a document. Sections of documents can be protected against alterations using the tools provided in the Review tab in Microsoft Office applications, as shown in Figure 7.4.

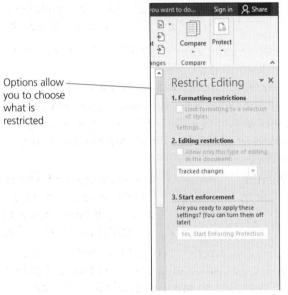

Options allow you to choose what is restricted

Figure 7.4 Restricting editing in Microsoft Office applications

Saving and exporting documents

Usually the proprietary, native format provided by an application is the best choice for saving a document. This will make sure that all the text, formatting, styles and embedded data are saved properly so that it can be easily retrieved when needed.

It may not be possible to use the application's native format when moving the document content

to, or extracting it for use in, another application. The destination application may not support the file format being used, in which case a different format must be used.

Open formats are used by a variety of software applications and can be used to export and transfer data between applications. Some open file formats that can be used by most word-processing and desktop-publishing applications are shown in Table 7.1.

Table 7.1 Open file formats that can be used by most word-processing and desktop-publishing applications

File extension	Meaning	Typically used to store
.rtf	rich text format	Word-processed documents
.txt	text	Unformatted text files
.pdf	portable document format	Formatted documents
.csv	comma separated values	Lists of data, for example for use in mail merge for simple lists

Which file format is used will depend on the software application being used at the time and what the user wants to do with the file or extracted data.

Using open file formats sometimes, but not always, causes the formatting of the document to change or be lost altogether.

Table 7.2 shows some strengths and weaknesses of the different file formats.

Table 7.2 Strengths and weaknesses of open file formats

File extension	Strengths	Weaknesses
.rtf	Most office applications can save and open files saved in this format.	Some formatting may be lost.
.txt	Only the text is saved, so the file size may be smaller than a word-processed document. Many applications can save and import text files, so this is useful for transferring text between packages.	Saving a file as text from a word processing package will lose most, if not all, of the formatting. Images and links will also be lost.
.pdf	Many applications can open and display PDF files. PDF files can be difficult to edit, so can be used to try and stop others altering your work.	PDF files can be difficult to edit, so are not useful for saving work that is being developed.
.csv	Most data-handling packages can import and export data as CSV files.	There is no information other than the raw data in a CSV file.

How to use presentation techniques

Text and objects

Text anchors

Text anchors are hyperlinks that, when clicked, send the user to a web page, to another document, to another slide in the show or even to another slide in a different slideshow.

Links can be created that start other applications or websites. Any object on a slide can have an action button added to it, as shown in Figure 7.5.

Options allow you to choose what is launched when the object is clicked or the mouse is moved over it

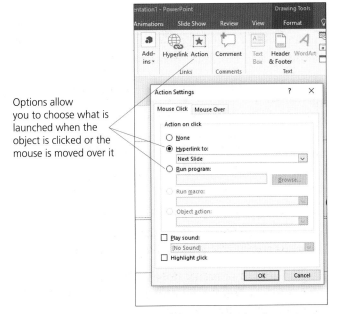

Figure 7.5 Setting what is launched by an action button

Images

Photographs, diagrams or drawings increase the impact of a presentation and convey information well.

Images should be optimised for use in a presentation using the image-editing tools found in graphics packages. Photographs can be edited to remove unwanted areas or artefacts, to add effects or text, or to be altered to suit the presentation.

Some drawing tools are available in Microsoft PowerPoint to allow you to layer, group and rotate images and drawings within your slides. Images and objects can be resized by dragging the corners of the object.

Some of the more useful tools for editing images include:

- Layering allows objects in the image to be individually edited, positioned or blended without affecting any of the other layers.
- Grouping objects in an image means the grouped objects are treated as a single object. Grouped objects can be moved around together.
- Cropping images allows unwanted parts of an image to be removed.
- Cutting takes out unwanted parts of the image.
- Flipping an image reverses it, as if you are looking at it in a mirror. Flipping is usually across the horizontal axis but can be on the vertical axis.
- Rotating an image turns the image as if it were stuck to a turning wheel. The rotation can be through any number of degrees of turn. Images are often rotated from the horizontal for artistic effect.
- Scaling an image changes its physical size. An image can be enlarged or reduced. Scaling changes the number of pixels in a bitmap image and will often change the quality of the image. If a vector image is scaled there should no change in the quality of the image.

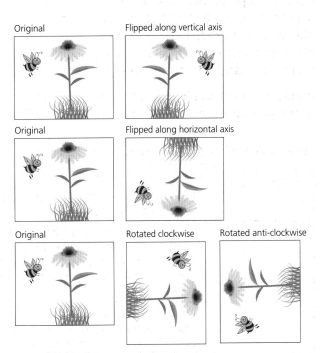

Figure 7.6 Flipping and rotating an image

Top tip

Make sure that you know the difference between flipping and rotation of images.

Slideshow management

Sound and video

Sound and video clips increase an audience's interest and can explain information in ways that text cannot. Video does not require a person to be able to read or even understand a language; they just watch.

When including a sound clip, you should choose whether to link it or embed it before you use it. Embedded sound files have to be in a format that the presentation or slideshow application can play and will increase the file size of the slideshow. Linked files have to available when required and may need additional software or sound systems to play them.

Sound files should be in the highest quality possible because they will be amplified so that the audience can hear them. Any background noises or distortion will be magnified and spoil the sound.

Video files can be large so embedding a video clip may not be possible. If the video is linked, it must – like other linked objects – always be available. Video clips should be of the highest quality obtainable and the size and resolution should be set so the whole audience can see the content clearly.

You must take into account any copyright restrictions that may apply when using sound and video that you have not created yourself.

Branching, linear and non-linear slideshows

Slideshows can be automated or controlled manually by the speaker. Manually controlling the slideshow gives the speaker flexibility as to when to change slides and the opportunity to skip slides or go back to earlier slides.

Branching slideshows allow users to make choices about where they go next in a slideshow, or have links that go to other slideshows from within a slideshow.

Linear slideshows go through the slides in a strict order and do not allow for any alternative routes.

Non-linear slideshows are like a website, where the slides have links to different slides and the user or speaker can choose which to go to next. There is also a set of navigation buttons to allow the user to go forward to the next slide and back to the previous slide. There should also be a Home slide to which all slides can return quickly using a Home link attached to an object. A Home action button should be inserted into the master slide so it appears on all slides.

A presentation to a large audience would use a slideshow that contains a variety of different media types – text, images, video, animations and sounds – and suitable mixes and transitions.

Speaker notes

Notes can be added to a slideshow to show the speaker important points that must be talked about when showing the slideshow to an audience. Speaker notes appear at the bottom of each slide and are not usually visible to the audience.

Speaker notes can be added using the Speaker Notes view and can be printed separately from the slideshow in Microsoft PowerPoint.

Careful use of speaker notes can enhance a presentation by reminding speakers of key points that must be mentioned.

Top tip

Electronic documents can be enhanced in ways that are not possible with paper documents. Colours can be changed depending on the display, text can move about, video and audio can be included. However, you must take care that your digital documents do not use too many different features or they will not look pleasing to the eye.

Study commercial documents, websites, mobile apps and websites on mobile devices to see how features are used on these. This will allow you to see what looks good and what does not.

Customising slideshows

All items and objects included in a presentation should be there to increase the impact for, or the understanding by, the audience of the information that is being presented. Any item or object that does not do this isn't needed.

Master pages

A master page or slide holds details that will appear on all the slides in a presentation. The formatting, fonts and content that are found in the master slide are automatically included on every slide.

Master slides should be created before any other slides so that the layout and content are set up before you edit any new slides. Any changes made to new slides will not be found in the master slide or other slides.

Templates

Templates are pre-set slide layouts that are provided by the software creator and included in the application, or are slide layouts that you have created and set as templates. Creating your own template for use gives you total control over how the slideshow appears. You can set background colours, themes and effects of your choice so that you don't have to edit each individual slide. Text placeholders can be used to allow different, personalised information to be added by users in a specific place on the slide. The name of the presenter and the date could be added using text placeholders.

Integrating with other applications

Using text in a presentation

Text can easily be added almost anywhere on a slide by creating a text box and typing the text in the box. The format of the text on the slide can be altered as required. The amount of text should be kept to a minimum and it should be large enough to see easily, as most people will not be able to read large amounts of small text.

Text can be imported from files so there is no need to retype it. The text in a presentation can also be exported for use in word-processing applications. This may be useful if you wish to give summaries to audiences in addition to handouts of the slides.

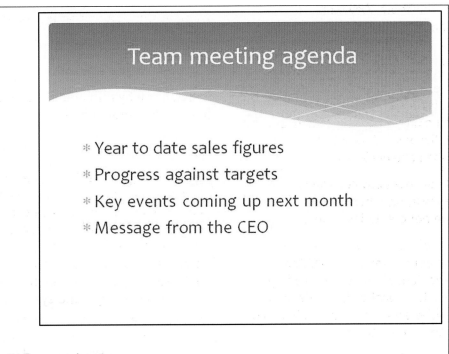

Figure 7.7 A presentation with speaker notes

Linking presentations with other applications

Links to other sections

You learned about linking presentations with other applications in Chapter 5, Section 5.1.

Objects can be linked to, or embedded in, a presentation.

Linked objects are updated when the source object is updated but require the source object always to be available for use. Charts and graphs from spreadsheets can be linked so that when the source data is updated the chart will automatically change to show the effects of the new data. This means that the data is always up to date and as accurate as possible.

Embedded objects become part of the slideshow presentation and are not automatically updated, but they are always available. Embedded objects have to be edited within the presentation. Embedded objects increase the file size of the presentation.

Launching websites and other applications

Showing a live website in your presentation is much more effective and engaging to an audience than a static screenshot. A screenshot may be out of date, while a live website will always show the latest version. Embedding a live website into a PowerPoint slide may require the use of third-party add-ins, but links can be created to open and show a website or other application from PowerPoint. This is done by inserting a hyperlink to the website or application into the object. The object can be any text, shape or image that you want to use for launch. When the object is clicked on, the link will launch the website or application.

Security of documents

The data in a slideshow can be secured in a number of ways. In Microsoft PowerPoint, permissions can set to restrict users from altering the presentation, as shown in Figure 7.8.

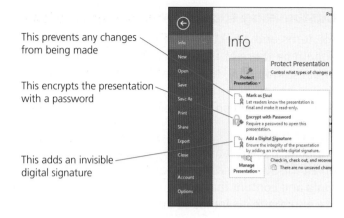

This prevents any changes from being made

This encrypts the presentation with a password

This adds an invisible digital signature

Figure 7.8 Setting permissions in Microsoft PowerPoint 2016

There are other ways to protect the data in your presentation. A slideshow can be exported as a PDF file or as images so that the data cannot be changed. These methods are useful when sending your presentations to others for review.

Saving and exporting slideshow presentations

Links to other sections

You learned about saving and exporting data between applications earlier in Section 7.2.

Slideshow presentations are best saved in the format associated with the software. Sometimes, however, exporting in a different format will enable the presentation to be sent to others to check or view, e.g. as a PDF or in a non-editable version.

Presenting information on websites

Information can be made available to very large audiences by using websites. Websites can be viewed on many different devices, ranging from desktop computers to smartphones. Web designers must take into account the different platforms that can be used. It is usual to make a basic website that can be displayed on older devices and then to enhance the pages for smartphones and tablets.

Using a website to present your information allows you to reach a wider audience than if you used traditional methods. The drawback of using a website to present complex information is the need to convert all the text, images and videos to be compliant with the requirements of HTML coding. Also, the display of information can be limited by the size of web pages and the need to ensure that it will display properly on mobile devices.

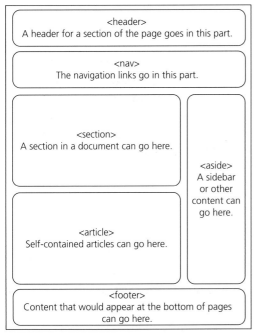

Figure 7.9 The parts of a basic web page, defined using HTML5 elements

HTML and CSS

Hypertext mark-up language (**HTML**) and cascading style sheets (**CSS**) are technologies that allow the world wide web to function as a method of distributing information. At the time of writing, the current versions are HTML5 and CSS3.

HTML describes the structure, make up and content of web pages. CSS describes how the layout, fonts and colours of documents are presented using HTML.

> **Key terms**
>
> **HTML (hyper-text mark-up language)** is used to place content on a website.
>
> **CSS (cascading style sheets)** are used to control the presentation of the content on a website.

HTML

HTML is used to give instructions to **web browsers** about how to display web pages and any multimedia content that is required on the pages. There are several components to HTML mark-up code that are necessary for displaying pages. HTML code tells the web browser what type of document is to be displayed, what items or elements are to be included and how to display the items.

> **Key term**
>
> **Web browsers** are designed to read HTML documents and to display them. Web browsers use HTML tags to determine how to display HTML documents.

HTML tags are used to determine how the web page should be displayed. Many tags are used in pairs, with one start tag and one end tag. Start tags are in brackets, for example <body>. End tags have a forward slash added after the opening bracket, for example </body>.

The HTML code shown below will create a simple web page as shown in Figure 7.10.

```
<!DOCTYPE html>

<html>

<head>

<title>A Simple Web Page</title>

<style>

body {background-color: yellow;}
h1 {color: blue;}

</style>

</head>

<body>

<h1>My Heading looks like this but I could change the font using a tag!</h1>

<p>I can start a new paragraph.</p>

This is some text on the page.

</body>

</html>
```

The table explains what the HTML code tells the web browser about the simple page so that it can display it.

HTML tag	What the tag does
<!DOCTYPE html>	States that the type of document is HTML5
<html>	Tells the browser that the HTML code starts here
<head>	Indicates the start of the header section of the HTML code
<title>A Simple Web Page </title>	Indicates the start, the content and the end of the page title that appears in the tab at the top of the browser
<style>body {background-color: yellow;} h1 {color: blue;} </style>	The <Style> and </Style> tags tell the web browser to interpret the code between them as CSS and to apply them to the HTML code. In this case the CSS sets the background colour of the page body to yellow and the colour of h1 to blue when the page is displayed in a browser
</head>	Indicates the end of the header section of the HTML code
<body>	Indicates the start of the body of the page
<h1>My Heading looks like this but I could change the font using a tag!</h1>	Indicates the start, the content and the end of the header on this page when displayed in a browser
<p>I can start a new para- graph.</p>	<p> tags indicate the start, the content and the end of paragraphs
</body>	Indicates the end of the HTML body
</html>	Tells the browser that the HTML code ends here

Only the content within the <body> </body> tags is displayed in the browser, so in Figure 7.10 the text 'This is some text on the page.' is displayed.

The 'head' section can be used to hold instructions to set styles within the web page using CSS.

Cascading style sheets

Cascading style sheets (CSS) are used to describe how the elements included in the HTML code are displayed on screen. Style sheets can be placed in the 'head' section and define the styles for that

Figure 7.10 A simple web page created using HTML

particular page only. The <style> tag can be used to define how other tags work on a page, for example:

```
<style>
h1 {color: blue;font-size: 54px }
</style>
```

This makes the h1 tag display the header in blue with a font size of 54px every time it is used on a page.

Style sheets can also be in line with the tag, but this loses most of the advantages of having style sheets, so should be used very rarely.

External CSS files are style sheets that are stored in files which can be loaded by many web pages, so a single CSS can control the layout of multiple web pages and even a whole website. Writing one CSS allows you to dictate how all of your web pages will look. The CSS controls the format of the pages and can describe where images go, the size of images, the fonts to be used for text and many more layout options. There are some strict rules about the content of CSS files, for example, there must be no HTML tags in an external CSS file. Usually, instructions in CSS are in blocks within { } brackets. This block will make the h1 tag display at 60px in size, be in blue and underlined:

```
h1 {
    font-size: 60px;
    color: blue;
    text-decoration: underline;
}
```

External CSS sheets can be written in any text editor but must be saved with the .css file extension. Every page that uses the external CSS file must have a reference to it using the <link> tag in the <head> section so that the browser knows where to find the file and what it is.

> **Top tips**
>
> When creating links to external style sheets in your web pages, make sure that you do not use a fixed reference to a specific folder. Use a 'relative reference' to ensure that if you move the site, the web pages will still be able to find the style sheets.
>
> Be very careful when using both internal and external style sheets on your pages. Sometimes you may wish to 'override' a style on a particular page, so remember that the last style for a tag that the web browser 'sees' will be the one used on that page. This also applies if you use more than one external style sheet: later styles override earlier ones.

The appearance of web pages

It is very important to make sure that your web pages look good to others, regardless of what computer device they are using to view them.

When creating your web pages, make sure that users are asked to test them so that they make comments and give feedback. Users should give feedback on how the pages look, referring to your use of fonts, colours, backgrounds, images and so on. They should also test the pages for usability and accessibility. These tests, and the feedback, can be used to improve your pages and to provide evidence that can be used in your reviews and evaluations.

Mobile technologies

If you wish your web pages to be viewed properly on a range of devices, including smartphones, then you need to consider the 'mobile web' when designing your pages. The 'mobile web' means the world wide web as viewed on mobile devices!

There are several ways to make sure that your web pages will be displayed properly on mobile devices. One way is to have a separate website to which mobile devices are redirected. Using a separate website means that you have to detect the type of device being used to view your pages, and that two websites have to be developed and maintained. Developing a separate website can be time-consuming and may result in you leaving out some aspects of your pages in case they don't display properly. Leaving out features because it is simpler to do so does not give the viewer a good experience.

Most modern mobile devices can handle the latest web technologies quite well, so having separate sites may not be necessary; it is better to let mobile devices decide how to display your website. One method is to optimise your website for use on mobile devices, and query the device from the server, or using code in your web pages, to find out the capabilities of the device before sending it the optimised content.

Responsive web design requires that a web page be able to discover what sort of device it is being displayed upon. A CSS3 module called 'Media queries' (called a media type in CSS2) is used in the header of an HTML document. It checks the device to find out what screen resolutions and screen sizes are available. It can then decide which style sheet and rules to use to display the web page. This allows a single web page to be properly displayed on different devices.

You can include a block of CSS rules in a media query and apply them to your HTML code depending on the conditions that you set. Media queries can check many aspects of a device, including orientation, resolution, and screen size.

An example media query process could choose versions of pages or make decisions on what or how to display content by checking the screen size of the device; then further style sheets or blocks of code could be used to set up the versions or change the output to the display accordingly (see Figures 7.11, 7.12 and 7.13).

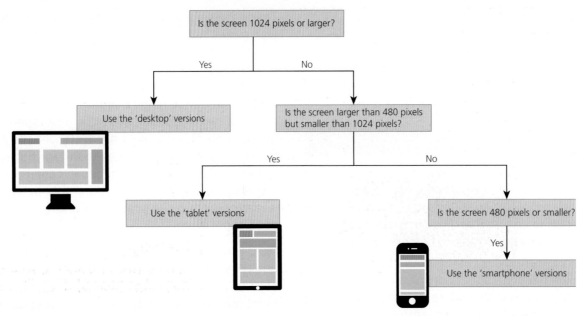

Figure 7.11 A CSS3 media query

An example would be to query the size of the screen so that suitable background colours can be used on different size screens for better viewing. A CSS3 media query is in the form:

```
@media (max-width: 767px) {
}
```

In this case the query is regarding screen size. Any further instructions in the curly brackets would only be carried out if the screen was 767 pixels or smaller.

Another example would be to move content so that it displays properly on different devices.

Most aspects of your web pages can be adjusted to make them more 'friendly' when used on mobile devices. When displaying pages on mobile devices, you could make sure that:

- the width of the page is adjusted to remove any white space from the sides, so that it does not show
- the width of any images is changed to fill the whole screen on the mobile device
- any input fields fill the whole screen so that users can easily see and use them
- only standard fonts are used so that text displays properly.

Responsive web design can also use a grid that is measured in units relative to the page size. This is used for each page so that the contents of each section of the grid can be moved around the page. The position of each section of the grid will depend on what device it is being displayed on. Desktop screens are in landscape orientation and large, while smartphone screens are portrait (or landscape, depending on how they are held) and small. Moving the sections of the page allows the elements to be displayed at their best. Any images that are used are flexible, so that they stay within their own grid whatever device they appear on.

Figure 7.12 Responsive web design

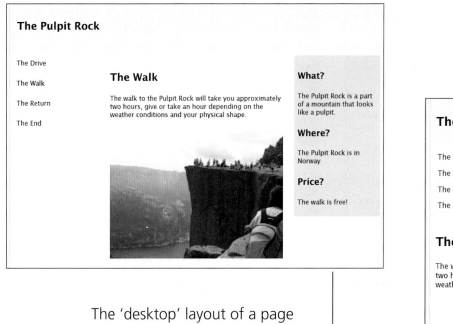

The 'desktop' layout of a page can be altered to the 'smartphone' layout by querying the size and orientation of the mobile device, then setting the styles accordingly.

Figure 7.13 Changing the layout for the size of screen

Top tip

As with all of your work, make sure that you have security measures in place to protect your work. This could include:

- using passwords to protect your original files
- setting access rights to prevent other people from altering your files
- converting any word-processed or desktop-published documents to a PDF format
- placing watermarks with your name on images
- putting copyright messages on your web pages so people can see that they are your work
- putting copyright messages in your source code as commented lines.

Usability and accessibility

Usability means how well, or easily, your product can be used by your users to carry out the tasks that the product was designed for.

Accessibility means making your products available and easy to use by persons with the widest possible range of abilities. People differ in their mobility, hearing, visual and thinking abilities, so products should be designed and created in such a way that anyone can use them as easily as possible. A well-designed product will allow all persons to access and use it without having to be specially modified.

Websites and products designed for mobile technology can be made accessible during the planning and design phases. Page layouts, choice of words and phrasing, font types and sizes, background and text colours, use of alternative text for images and many more aspects should be considered.

Blogs

Blogs are a good way of providing information that is up to date and concise. Blogs also stimulate conversations between people as others can leave comments or update information. The most useful aspect of using blogs is that you can include presentations, video clips and images, which can be linked to social media. The drawback is that blogs are really only useful for data or information that changes and needs to be continually updated.

Social media

There are a number of social media websites available for you to use to present the information from your project. Whichever one you choose, you need to create an account specifically for your project as you do not want any of your personal accounts to be used for this purpose. If you must provide a few details about yourself then you must make sure that this is done very carefully to ensure your safety; it is probably best not to put very much at all. Posts of your project results could include videos, photographs, other images, drawings and charts to make the site more interesting to others. You can add links to your documentation – in the form of PDFs of your work – or add hashtags or other links so that others can find your work when they search for a topic.

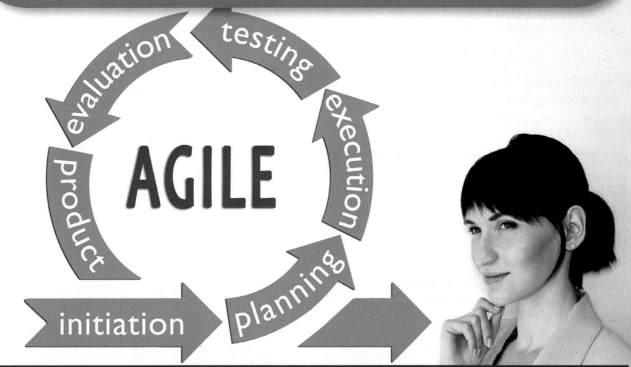

About this chapter

During a project life cycle it is important to review the progress at every phase. Reviews will show up areas that could be improved and action should be taken on the points raised in the reviews. Further reviews should be carried to check the results of the actions.

In this chapter, you will learn how to review your project as it progresses and how to record your findings.

You will also learn how to review your solution against the original plans and designs

Chapter content

8.1 How to carry out and document an iterative review

8.1 How to carry out and document an iterative review

Top tip

You are expected to carry out reviews when creating your data handling and communication products. Be sure to keep records of these reviews, and include your findings in your evaluation.

Phase reviews

 Key terms

Iterative review Carrying out a review, making changes as a result of the review, and then carrying out another review and making more changes. The process is repeated until the solution is as perfect as it can get.

Project life cycle Has the phases: initiation; planning; execution; evaluation.

Phase reviews should be carried out at the end of each stage of the **project life cycle**. The reviews should show whether or not the phases have produced what was expected.

A review could use a checklist with a series of questions about each phase. The checklist can be shown to the prospective user or project developer, or you can use it to check how your project is progressing.

Links to other sections

You learned about the phases of the project life cycle in Chapter 1, Section 1.1.

Phase review of initiation

The review of the initiation phase must check that the questions that were asked at the beginning have been answered.

A simple checklist with tick boxes can be used. Some questions that could be asked on your checklist include:

● Has the end product been identified?	Yes	No
● Can the project objectives easily be measured?	Yes	No
● Has the timescale for the project been decided?	Yes	No
● Has the target age group been identified?	Yes	No
● Has the software to be used been decided?	Yes	No

Your list of questions should cover these and other aspects, to check that your initial planning is on track and that the project can be carried out.

You must be sure that all the questions have been answered honestly and to your complete satisfaction. Good questions to ask yourself are 'Is this project possible?' or 'Can I do this project in the time I have been given?'

If the answers to some of your questions are 'No' or they create some doubt, then you will have to go back to redo or rethink the work.

Any actions that you have to take must also be recorded and justified. The questions should then be asked again to check that the actions have worked.

If some of the questions still cannot be answered or have been answered with 'no', then it is essential that you go back and amend or correct your work again so that your questions can be successfully answered. Leaving questions unanswered or showing a 'no' when it should be 'yes' gives the impression that your work is incomplete. When all the questions have been answered and recorded, you should ask if the project is ready to progress to the next phase. It is important that you do not move on to the next phase until all the amendments or corrections pinpointed by your reviews have been properly dealt with. If the review is not carried out thoroughly and honestly then the project will not succeed.

Your documentation of the reviews must include copies of questionnaires or surveys that you have undertaken. Also include references to, or details of, all other research that you did.

Phase review of the planning phase

The review of the planning phase must check that the questions that were asked at the beginning have been answered.

A simple checklist with tick boxes can be used. Some questions that could be asked on your checklist include:

- Have all the tasks been identified?   Yes   No
- Are the timescales reasonable?   Yes   No
- Have the tasks been put in the order in which they need to be completed?   Yes   No
- Has the critical path been identified?   Yes   No
- Has sufficient/appropriate contingency time been allowed?   Yes   No
- Has the project endpoint been identified?   Yes   No
- Are there measurable success criteria?   Yes   No

Your checklist will include other possible questions, such as identifying milestones, to check that the planning is suitable to allow the project to move on to the next phase.

There may be questions that require more in-depth answers and you should include these in your phase review documentation.

This review of the planning phase will make sure that the project plan is complete. It will show that the project can be delivered on time and you can make a decision about carrying on with the project.

Phase review of the execution phase

The review of the execution phase is used to check that the project is complete. The execution phase is often the longest phase and will consist of numerous tasks. It is sensible to review each task as it is being carried out and when it is completed. This will avoid you getting to end of the project and discovering that your solution does not work as you intended.

The reviews of each of the tasks will include testing of the solution and its component parts as it is being created. A spreadsheet or a database must be thoroughly tested as it is being created

and as a final product to ensure that it works as you intended and meets the requirements set out in the planning phase. You must also review the creation of reports, slideshows and other documentation and record your findings and changes that you made during their creation for the presentation section.

Phase reviews should take place after each of the different project phases, i.e. initiation/planning, data handling and information presentation. These will form part of the evidence for Assessment Task 3a.

You must record the testing and the actions taken as a result of testing, and the retesting carried out during the development of the data-handling phase.

It is best to review and document your work as you do it. This will make sure that you achieve the higher marks when your work is assessed.

A checklist of the items to include will help you organise reviews and evaluations. Some possible items to include on your checklist are:

- a list of the tests carried out on each of your products and their component parts, e.g. the formulas in spreadsheets, the mail merge templates using data from your spreadsheets or databases, or the feedback from your templates for documents with house styles
- a list of the changes you made when creating slideshows
- the results of testing the navigation controls around any interactive slideshows you have created
- feedback from people you have asked to review your work
- a summary checklist to check that you have actually tested every aspect of your products.

Top tip

- Record *all* tests and *all* changes that you make to your product as you go along.
- Record the results of the tests.
- Record the reasons why you carried out the tests and why you made the changes.

Final evaluation

Links to other sections

You learned about evaluation of the project in Chapter 1, Section 1.1.

At this point, the project will be almost complete. The final products will have been completed and any required documentation will ready. This phase is often called the evaluation of the project.

The final evaluation during this stage will:

- check that the project success criteria, set out in the initial planning, have been met
- check that the user requirements, created in the initiation phase, have been met
- review any deviations from original plans and justify them
- compare the original planning documents with the final outcomes of the product

- review whether or not the project tasks and the whole project have been completed on time.

This review documentation must also include the effects on the project of the constraints identified in the initial phases. This should include references to:

- the software application used
- the tools and features of the software used
- the techniques used to develop the solution
- any incompatibilities between software applications and computer systems that affected the choices made.

A final review should also include how your solution can be maintained and suggestions for improvements to your solution, for example further developments or updates that might need to be made as techniques improve or software is upgraded.

Glossary

Absolute cell referencing
Cell references with a $ sign in front of the column and row references – e.g. =SUM($A$1:$D$1) – do not change when the function or formula is copied or moved.

Access rights Control over who has access to a computer system, folder, files, data and/or information.

ANPR Automatic Number Plate Recognition.

Asset log A list of all the resources used in a project.

Bias An unfair inclination towards or against a person or group of people.

Buffering When an internet connection is too slow to show a resource in real time.

Caption The title or label of a diagram, drawing or photograph.

Check boxes These show a Yes/No choice – ticked when Yes, empty (clear or unticked) when No.

Client brief The document that details the client's requirements.

Closed question A question where there is only a set number of answers to be chosen, for example for 'Can you ride a bicycle?' the answers would be either 'Yes' or 'No'.

Comment A note attached to a piece of text.

Concurrent Tasks that can be completed at the same time.

Content table A list at the front of a book or report showing what is in the book or report.

Contingency Time in a project plan that has no tasks assigned. This is used if tasks are not completed on time to make sure the project still meets the final deadline.

Critical path The sequence of tasks that shows the shortest time taken for completion of a project.

Critical path method A planning technique that aims to prevent time bottlenecks by showing the critical and non-critical tasks for the completion of a project.

CSS (cascading style sheets) are used to control the presentation of the content on a website.

CSV file A type of plain text file where the fields are separated by commas and the records are separated by carriage returns.

Data Raw facts and figures before they have been processed.

Data dictionary A description of the structure, contents and format of a spreadsheet or a database. The relationships within the database are also included.

Defamation of character Making a false statement about someone that causes them harm.

Delimiter A separator between values. The delimiter in this list of fruit is a comma: apples, pears, oranges.

Dependency A dependent task is one that cannot be started until a previous, specified task has been completed.

Distribution channels The methods that can be used to share information by individuals, organisations or businesses.

Encryption code/key A set of characters, a phrase or numbers that is used when encrypting or decrypting data or a file.

Encryption software Software that is used to encrypt a file or data.

Endnote An item at the end of a book or report containing further information about the content in the text. Usually referenced with a number.

Erroneous data Data that is not acceptable to a computer system.

Extreme data Data that is on the boundary between data that is acceptable and data that is not acceptable to a computer system. Extreme data should be accepted by a computer system as it is still valid data.

Field An individual data item within a record. Each field has a unique name and contains a single data type.

Footer The section at the bottom of a page that contains information that appears on every page.

Footnote An item at the bottom of a page with further information about the content on a page. Usually referenced with a number.

Formula A spreadsheet formula carries out calculations on numbers using cell addresses and mathematical operators. It can use the ready-made functions.

Function Spreadsheet functions are ready-made, built-in tools for manipulating data.

Gantt chart A visual method of showing the proposed timing of each task needed to complete a project.

GIGO Garbage In, Garbage Out.

Goal What you wish to be able to do.

Header The section at the top of a page that contains information that appears on every page.

House style A description of the standards for text and graphics in all of the documents to be produced or used by a company.

HTML (hyper-text mark-up language) is used to place content on a website.

Index An alphabetical list at the end of a book or report that helps readers to find items of content.

Integrated document A document featuring components from other documents, including spreadsheets, databases or web links.

Interaction How the phases of the project life cycle link together.

Internet of things The interconnection via the internet of computing devices embedded in everyday objects, enabling them to send and receive data.

Interviewee The person answering the questions.

Interviewer The person asking the questions.

Iteration The repeating of a phase. Each repetition of a phase, when amendments will be made, is called an iteration. The results of an iteration are used as the starting point of the next.

Iterative review Carrying out a review, making changes as a result of the review, and then carrying out another review and making more changes. The process is repeated until the solution is as perfect as it can get.

Key-word analysis Analysing the client brief to determine and highlight the important aspects of the project.

Milestone A given point in time when a task is expected to be started or completed.

MOOC A Massive Open Online Course is an online course with unlimited numbers of students and open access via a website.

Normal data Data that is acceptable to a computer system.

Objective What you actually have to do or carry out.

Open question Allows the person completing the questionnaire to give a detailed answer in their own words.

Option boxes (or radio buttons) Allow users to select only one choice from two, mutually exclusive options. The choice is either 'this one' or 'that one', not both.

Password A set of characters that allows access to a computer system.

Permissions A set of attributes that determine what a user can do with files and folders, for example read, write, edit or delete.

PERT Program Evaluation Review Technique.

Project life cycle Has the phases: initiation; planning; execution; evaluation.

Project manager The person who is in overall charge of the project. They do not carry out any of the development tasks associated with the project but manage the tasks, people and resources needed.

Project scope Breaking down a project into manageable tasks.

Public authorities Include government departments, the NHS, state schools and the police force.

Query A way of interrogating and manipulating data within a database. A query has rules that filter to the specific data needed.

Range A group of cells in a spreadsheet.

Rank order Requires the person completing the questionnaire to compare a list of the same type of items. The items are then ranked, for example from 1 to 10 where 1 is very important and 10 is least important.

Rating Requires the person completing the questionnaire to compare different items. The items are then ranked, for example from 1 to 10 where 1 is very important and 10 is least important.

Real-time data (RTD) Data that is delivered immediately after it has been collected.

Record A collection of data about a single item, such as a single student or customer. Each record must be unique.

Relative cell referencing Cell references – e.g. =SUM(A1:D1) – that change when the function or formula is copied or moved.

Resources The things needed to complete the project. These may include hardware, software and the different specialist roles such as programmers and testers.

RFID Radio Frequency Identification Tags can use radio frequency to transfer data from the tags to a computer system, for example to allow access to a room.

Risk A possible action or inaction to/in the project that slows it down or prevents it being completed.

Risk mitigation Creating options and actions to reduce risks and threats to the project.

Section An area of a page that has its own formatting.

Strong password A password usually consisting of six or more characters that are a mixture of upper- and lower-case letters, numbers and symbols so that it is very difficult to guess. Not all computer systems allow all characters to be used.

Sum To add up.

SWOT Analysis to find out the Strengths, Weaknesses, Opportunities and Threats of/to a project.

Table Contains data about 'things', for example students, customers or orders. Each table has a unique name and contains data held in records.

Text file A plain text file. For importing into Excel, a text file uses tabs or spaces as delimiters for fields and carriage returns to separate records. A file using tabs may be called a TSV file.

Track Changes A system of making changes to text but retaining the original text so that changes can be seen and, if required, reversed.

Validation Checks that the data being entered into a computer system is sensible and reasonable. Validation checks the data against pre-set rules.

Verification A check to see whether the data being entered into a computer system is identical to the source from which it came.

VoIP Voice over Internet Protocol.

Watermark A pattern printed or inserted across an image or document.

Web browsers are designed to read HTML documents and to display them. Web browsers use HTML tags to determine how to display HTML documents.

Workflow What task is dependent on another, what task has to be completed before moving on to the next and which tasks can be completed at the same time as others.

WYSIWYG What You See Is What You Get.

Index